ADRIAN LUCHINI

CONTEMPORARY
WORLD
ARCHITECTS

ADRIAN LUCHINI

Foreword by
Enric Miralles

Introduction by
Lauren Kogod

Essay by
Adrian Luchini

Concept and Design by
Lucas H. Guerra
Oscar Riera Ojeda

ROCKPORT PUBLISHERS
GLOUCESTER, MASSACHUSETTS

First published in the United States of America by:
Rockport Publishers, Inc.
33 Commercial Street
Gloucester, Massachusetts 01930
Telephone: 978-282-9590
Fax: 978-283-2742

Distributed to the book trade and art trade in the United States of America by
North Light Books, an imprint of F & W Publications
1504 Dana Avenue
Cincinnati, Ohio 45207
Telephone: 513-531-2222

Other distribution by Rockport Publishers, Inc.

ISBN 1-56496-503-1
10 9 8 7 6 5 4 3 2 1
Manufactured in China.

Cover photograph: Piku Residence by Balthazar Korab
Back cover photographs: (Top) Maritz-Starek Residence by Sam Frentress
(Bottom) Cooper Bauer Apartment by Adrian Luchini
Back flap photograph: Adrian Luchini by J. F. Photography
Pages 1-3 photographs: Piku Residence by Balthazar Korab

Graphic Design: Lucas H. Guerra/Oscar Riera Ojeda
Layout: Oscar Riera Ojeda
Composition: Hunha Lee

CONTENTS

Foreword

BY ENRIC MIRALLES

Among the working notes presented simultaneously with his works, the architect tries to reveal the most intimate aspect of his

task ... that which is most specific ... most precise.

Adrian introduces there subjective impressions, reflections, readings ...

He talks to us about the way his architecture is linked to his vital experiences:

architecture as a personal journey through its own paths.

as a tool to understand what happens around us.

The architect is not someone who solves the problem of representing an institution, but rather someone who returns its status to

the most humane of its origins.

The project of the Sixth Church of Christ, Scientist explains this very well. There is great tenderness in that project:

I marvel at Adrian's conviction to "get something" out of there!

That effort to reveal—of difficult translation—is clearly one of the pursuits in

Adrian's work ...

There is something of a personal challenge ...

Something like a blind impulse ...

Perhaps this impulse, this action, demonstrates how his sketches are comfortable among those of the contemporary Viennese

architects ...

The line quality obtained by the refined condition of his

gesture ... scratches the extremely

hard surface ....

That surface where proposals are constructed,

to "get something" out of the difficulties ...

For that reason his projects rest on an edge, an horizon

gradually darkening at the place where vision converges ...

And in that obscurity precise forms appear ...

I admire his project in Boston. I believe it has set the tone for many of his works.

This identification between his activities as architect with life itself ...

is also found in his teaching.
The professor uses the same sharp pencil to expose the students' works.

Adrian becomes a useful instrument . . .
He allows his drawings to follow the intuitions of his students as well as his clients' requests.
But these actions always lead toward his personal territory: a precise and delineated vision of
architecture.

Adrian—and this is wonderful—is thoroughly immersed in the projects he crafts. Anything else is uninteresting for him.

And in spite of that, the other day, when I asked one of my students at Harvard:

who has been your best professor? . . .

(A useful question when it is necessary to get closer to your acquaintance through a common friend)

the student mentioned Adrian's name.

And why? I asked

"Because he took my projects as if they were his own", he replied.
(What might also be a criticism to my distant attitude.)

It is important to realize that Adrian is interested in a very concrete form of architecture: his has a generic quality to it . . .

It makes me think that the only possible architecture is that which is so precise, so personal , intense and identified with its author,

defined by the concrete demands of a commission . . .

An architecture that from a specific situation gradually becomes a constellation where all of us reflect.

Sixth Church of Christ, Scientist (left):
Window display of biblical readings,
through a big "slice" on the wall that
peels off to the inside. KDNL, St. Louis
(center): the actual depth of the corridor
is distorted by a slanted wall decreasing
in height from one end of the corridor
to the other. Shaffer-Landick Residence,
St. Louis (right): the window detail
shows the intersection of the existing
house and the addition .

Introduction

BY LAUREN KOGOD

DRAWING SPACE WITH LINES

There is an extended-exposure photograph of Picasso in which the artist "draws" the figure of a bull with a flashlight in real, three-dimensional space on an imaginary picture plane. He literally draws the bull in the space between himself and the photographer. Evidently neither Picasso nor the photographer can see the bull; it will emerge later on the print in the darkroom. Picasso can see it in his mind's eye and he traces the figure out by memory, simultaneously creating and remembering it. The photograph is a testament to Picasso's ability to draw the complete figure of the bull without seeing what he is drawing; it is a testament to the pleasure or the significance of that ephemeral moment in which Picasso has conjured this image out of air and onto the air with a beam of light. The gesture of Picasso's arm drawing the bull is preserved in the image, as is the length of time measured or required by the drawing. In this sense, Picasso shows that, like Jackson Pollock, he is an "action painter," whose work bears the legible traces of the physical act of its creation: the gesture and the figure are the same.

Adrian Luchini's work brings this photograph to mind because its primary program is the persistent attempt to create space out of expressive and almost physically gestural lines that clearly are the lines of a free-hand draftsman. Again and again in his drawings and built work, a nervous or taut bundle of individual lines coalesces into spatial figures and conjures spaces with ephemeral boundaries simultaneously from air and in air. One has the sense that Luchini attempts to draw in space and to create space by the physical act of drawing. Lines—and the planes that result from the three-dimensional projection of lines—are folded into and onto themselves in order to invent space and to promise more space. The folding of lines generates a complexity and intensity of buildable space. This operation of folding lines and planes also inherently creates doubled spaces-within-spaces, both conceptual and perceptual, but not always habitable (beginning with the folded window of the Schaeffer-Landick addition).

In his early projects, most of which are renovations, lines were drawn through existing spaces to form horizontal or diagonal paths of circulation, material edges, unexpected sources of light, or double-sided functions (the horizontally-folded TV-station corridor wall, the Maritz-Starek stair, the display wall and interior partitions at Sixth Church of Christ, Scientist). In his larger and later projects (the remarkably consistent group of houses), lines are extruded into planes that delaminate, rather than delimit, interior from exterior space and interior spaces from one another. The significant architectural effects in this group of projects are invested along the long edges of programmatic bars: in almost all the houses, for example, unruly stairs or other events—usually circulation — slip alongside or in and out of the primary volume, testing and irritating its surface "skin." These delaminated paths test the interior status of the edges by offering long views parallel to the primary bar, extricating the inhabitant from within the building while one is still inside it. Often glazed surfaces fold in on themselves so interior views cross exterior spaces, causing a strangely self-referential, mirroring effect. In his largest and most recent projects, Luchini's interest has focused on the roof planes. These,

too, perform operations of folding, splitting, and delamination. From some points of view the roofs appear as a thin line, edge, or seam; from other vantage points they are bent or folded planes.

These projects maintain some of the indeterminate and gestured formal quality of freehand studies. Apparently unfinished trajectories and abrupt endings imply partially erased or incomplete sketches. Bent volumes are formed as often by short, brittle lines that have been built up over a series of sketches as by elastic and fluid ones. These curved or bent lines are constituted by the hand of the draftsman tracing over his previous lines. But each successive generation of representation is less tenuous and more emphatic than the next: edges indeterminate in the sketches become more confident when translated into computer drawings and then become definite when built. The nature and quality of the authorial hand is transformed from the freehand sketch to the computer drawing because, while the computer traces the intentions of the hand, it also reifies its gestures. At the same time, the computer makes it possible to propose these eccentric, gestural, and irregular forms. The computer can calibrate the precise measurements required for construction documents. The precision of computer drafting allows something of the ambiguous effect of the sketch to be maintained in the final form.

In light of the program of lines drawn in space, many of Luchini's freehand drawings appear coincident with the computer perspectives because of his consistent preference for the wire-frame drawing to more conventional, opaque, and therefore "realistic," representations. The wire-frame drawings present the voided architectural form and the space it occupies simultaneously as part of the same continuum. But the reader of this kind of drawing can only focus on one of the simultaneous images at a time: if one focuses on the gestural *lines*, the building is transparent and its space is continuous with the space around and through it. If, on the other hand, a reader conceptually makes the building opaque, the lines are read as the edges of *planes* and one sees the building emerge as a definite figure, discrete from the surrounding space. In this latter case, the building occupies a specific and palpable place in space. The quality or character of space is different in the two readings: in the opaque reading, laws of gravity apply. In the transparent reading, space—usually already considered immaterial—is further dematerialized. The status of both the architectural objects and space oscillates in these drawings: opaque or transparent, planes or lines, representational, palpable, and inhabitable space, or conceptual and immaterial space.

In their canonic essay on transparency, Colin Rowe and Robert Slutzky distinguished between physical transparency (one can see through it) and the condition of conceptual or "phenomenal" transparency. In the latter, drawn from an interpretation of paintings used to read two projects by Le Corbusier, a series of receding parallel planes were suggested by the articulation of edges, surfaces, and other formal cues, adding conceptual layers of space and depth to the actual built space. The mutual exclusivity of Rowe and

Piku Residence, Detroit. Sequence of images showing the relationship of the view (landscape) with the frame (architecture).

Slutzky's categories "literal" and "phenomenal" was extended when, in the 1970s, Bernard Tschumi outlined the opposing catgories "the experience of space" and "the idea of space." Tschumi theorized breaking this binary opposition, proposing the possibility of conceiving and experiencing space simultaneously, a radical idea. Luchini's drawings reply to the conflation of these two sets of propositions. His transparent perspective drawings bring the two mutually exclusive categories into a rapid oscillation, never quite crystallizing into the impossible synthetic third term.

The conceptual program indicated by the dematerialization of objects and space is underscored by the highly distorted views of the projects that Luchini often chooses to present. Usually architects are careful to construct and show those images that indicate with as much fidelity as possible the actual form, appearance, and experience of an architectural project as it will eventually be built. It is often assumed that the more "realistic" the renderings, the more "persuasive" they are and the more useful in evaluating the building that is (assumed to be) the end-product of the process of architectural design. That Luchini is interested in these drawings as autonomous works and not as communicative devices to help in the "translation" of drawings into buildings is pretty clear. And this parallel research in drawing or, more properly stated, this interest in the autonomy of the "architectural" drawing sites Luchini in a specific cultural and historical moment. Although Daniel Libeskind was his studio critic at the GSD for only one semester, the influence on Luchini seems strong in encouraging speculative research focused on the inner vision and in questioning the conventions of architectural representation.

The architectural work of Adrian Luchini is purely formal research, generated from his own previous architectural projects and from his dedicated work in drawing and monoprints—plumbing the inner vision. All architects draw, but not all architects do unmotivated freehand drawings—which are ends in themselves—as Luchini does. Are Luchini's drawing and architecture the same path of research? Sometimes these images belong to his architectural work and sometimes they do not. Even when they do—such as the freehand images you will find among the project "documentation" or "representation" in this book—the drawings often indicate no material or perceptual quality of the work as it would be built. Some of these drawings do not, in fact, present their "idea of space" at all. In this sense, they are not even representations. At most, we can read a psychological quality in the drawings attached to specific projects ranging across a broad emotional spectrum from a dense, almost claustrophobic, and urban intensity to a tenuous or desolate emptiness that suggests an air of troubled solitude. The inclusion of a human figure in many of these is the sole means by which this psychological projection can be read, giving a sense of potential inhabitation to the lines. Similarly, Luchini's written texts are not informative descriptions (you get no useful information from them) but are word-images that, like the freehand drawings, provide psychological portraits for the projects. One is about "a pause," another about "a strip-tease," and so on. The words are also declarations of intended emotional effects. Luchini supplements his formal architectural research with emotional and psychological inquiry.

Maritz-Starek residence—the stair is also a diving board, and it is, in its form and position, the embodiment of a jump in motion. The choice of stainless steel is adequate for its sturdiness and thinness, suggesting a minimally perceptible condition.

Piku Residence, Bloomfield Hills, Michigan. The fireplace, positioned in front of the window, captures the sunset, making its onyx surface to glow, thus echoing the presence of the fire from the hearth (right). Shaffer-Landick Residence addition, Saint Louis, Missouri: The articulation between the existing and the new registers the intrusion of eastern light, literally carving out the mass—an occasion to place two windows, one for the new space (mud room) and another for the renovated kitchen (opposite page).

The status of these psychological portraits is, however, somewhat ambiguous. They might be emotional effects intended for each project, or effects imagined for different moments within each project. Or they could reflect Luchini's own state when he drew them. Can an emotional state (or the emotional state of the author) be projected into architectural work and made palpable to the eventual inhabitant, as a range of architects from Boullée to some members of the Art Nouveau movement had hoped? We can on one hand imagine with these drawings that Luchini is focusing exclusively on his own inner vision; but we can also understand him to be projecting and choreographing the experience of his audience. In support of the first reading, Walter Benjamin wrote in "The Task of the Translator" that, although art "posits man's physical and spiritual existence" it is never "concerned with his response. No poem is intended for the reader, no picture for the beholder, no symphony for the listener." That is, the artist assumes the existence of an audience but does not concern him- or herself with its experience. The audience members benefit in that they watch (see, read, listen to, etc.) the artist's inner struggle and personal, conceptual research.

If I remember that photograph of Picasso correctly, however, the artist is looking directly into the camera, not at his own drawing. He regards us watching him draw as if he is acting a part rather than simply drawing. He may not be choreographing or controlling our responsive experience, but the direction of his gaze makes his concern for our existence very clear. He is conjuring this bull out of thin air like a magician for us, after all, not for himself. Luchini, too, draws in space in order for us to see his inner vision. The work becomes more real for him when he sees the psychological effects and the spatial oscillations reflected in our apprehension. That the gesture of his hand is retained in the built work is the articulate testament to his desire that we see the active process by which he draws spatial figures.

Essay

BY ADRIAN LUCHINI

BOXING RITUALS

ROUND ONE

There are no words here. There is also an absence of exclamation; all you hear are footsteps, their rhythm uneven but steady. But the journey is incomplete, populated, and fragmented. No specific stages, no clear chapters, only a bundle of recollections that will never amount to full phrases. Why? I reside in this question, as I am sure many more have, and plenty do. To describe a professional trajectory today is to give up, to abdicate that intimacy that can only be captured in the realm of the work itself, never through language. The work is inexplicable, it is important to say it up front. What informs it, what authorizes it, has either been absorbed by the work's proper domain, or eluded it forever.

I draw what has shaped me, from the early days, full of dust in Argentina to the cacophony of adulthood in the United States, from the simplicity of an implacable horizon line—"lethal horizon"—to the protocols of a profession increasingly confusing and more and more difficult, a cartography of pure desire and constant resistance. These works are always in the company of shadows. Never pure, their discrete identities simply reveal an instant of pleasure, intensely sought and seldom achieved. To be an architect today amounts to a very difficult task. It is more realistic to introduce myself as a survivor who has attempted various routes, from the small practice with a friend (Dirk Denison of Chicago), to the hidden complexity of the Midwest (Thomas Schwetye of St. Louis), to the extensive entanglement of the corporate world and its multiple agendas (HOK) to the paradoxical world of engineering, billability, and construction (Sverdrup). My hands hurt.

ROUND TWO

The projects have evolved through a couple of common goals.

Escape, momentarily, the voices that speak to you.

Inhabit instead the first traces of the desire that inform the project.

Avoid shortcuts and misleading paths; go beyond the predictable.

Listen to the multiple voices that too often attempt to silence the architectural, attend to their legislative demand, and move on.
The project's identity might be wrapped in them, but is seldom found there; they are the patina that affects their constructibility
and common sense, nothing more and nothing less. Keep moving, instead, until a true dialogue is opened up and there are no
more antagonisms between you and it, no more discrepancies, and only full associations between ideas, intentions, code, schedule,
budget, technique, and gesture. At that point, the rituals become a dance, and your adversary is your ally, all these forces seeking
a common end. The bell rings again.

ROUND THREE, FINAL

Gather your thoughts, express the necessary words of gratitude, and disappear. What always matters is not your presence, but the
opposite: the ability to gradually recede, in order to allow the work to speak its own discourse. If the encounter was successful,
the echo of your footsteps might resonate even after everyone has left.

Adrian Luchini, monoprints (from left
to right): *The Miracle, The Ritual, Study
for a Crucifixion*, and *The Architect's
House*. In these studies, gesture and
condition are always one and the
same, making explicit the desire to
illustrate action and message.

Monologues, Dialogues ▶

...Where one seeks for the moment when word and action become a single expression: shared, discovered, but never familiar. These projects evidence a process where the fundamental terms that inform them are never anticipated, where it is paramount to delay the emergence of a specific image, where the interlocutor is almost exclusively the drawing that appears intuitively, relegating any other form of description: where desire and impulse are seen as the only necessary point of departure.

Cooper Bauer Apartment

BOSTON, MASSACHUSETTS   with Dirk Denison

At the moment of the intervention, nothing moves. The duration of a single gesture (once found) provokes a delay in all the assumptions with which one starts working, be they programmatic, technical, conceptual: every one of them recedes. And the project begins there. As the few lines accommodate their own demands within the given boundaries, they establish new limits, or reiterate former ones. And sometimes they are barely able to affirm their permanence, as if doubting their own (proper) position:

intimate or distant
intrusive or circumspect
tangible or ethereal . . .

The rest is well known, and quickly occupied by that which is familiar: from the name (bedroom, closet, stair) to the construction detail. By now the gesture becomes an entity whose predicament is reiterated, protected from adversity, and finally released to the course of its own existence and destiny.

ıne stairs connecting the three levels in the atrium appear as a jump, or as an indication of multiple vectors of sight bouncing off the walls while ascending. The conscious transparency of the stairs helps convey the notion of mobility.

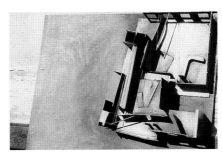

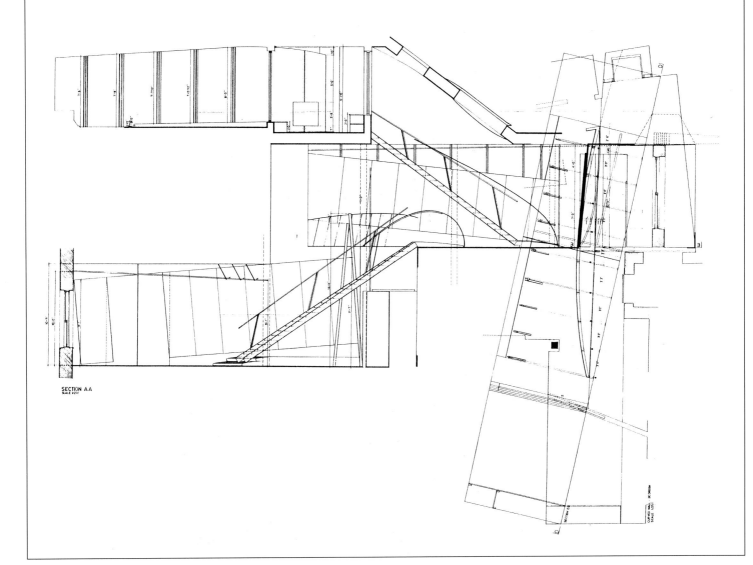

SECTION AA
SCALE 1/2"1'

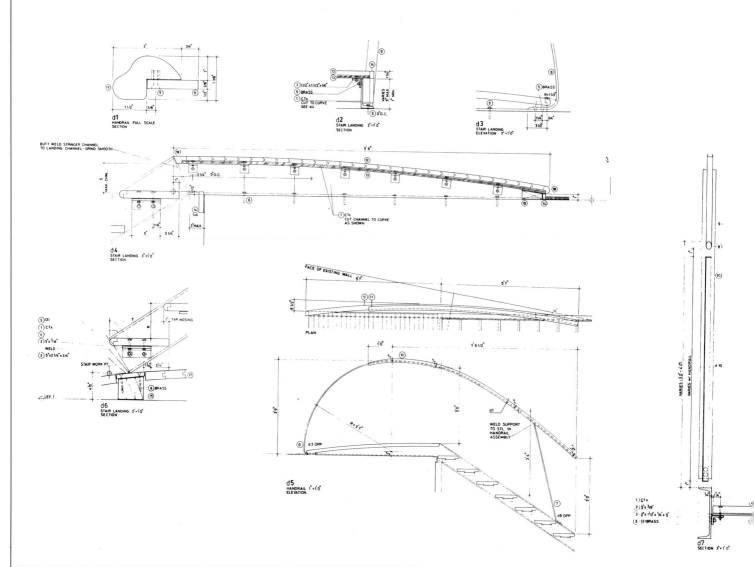

d1
HANDRAIL FULL SCALE
SECTION

d2
STAIR LANDING   3"=1'0"
SECTION

1 1/2" x 1 1/2" x 1/4"
BRASS
C7x
CUT TO CURVE
SEE d4

d3
STAIR LANDING
ELEVATION   3"=1'0"

BRASS
R=1 1/2"

BUTT WELD STRINGER CHANNEL
TO LANDING CHANNEL - GRIND SMOOTH

d4
STAIR LANDING   3"=1'0"
SECTION

C7x
CUT CHANNEL TO CURVE
AS SHOWN

5) (2)
1) C7x
4)
2) 5"x 3/8"
WELD
2) 5"x 2 1/4"x 3/4"

STAIR WORK PT.

d6
STAIR LANDING   3"=1'0"
SECTION

1" TYP. NOSING

BRASS

FACE OF EXISTING WALL

PLAN

d5
HANDRAIL   1"=1'0"
ELEVATION

R = 3'4"

d3 OPP

d1

WELD SUPPORT
TO STL. IN
HANDRAIL
ASSEMBLY

d9 OPP

d10

1) C7x
2) 5"x 3/8"
3) 2"x 1 1/2"x 1/16" x 5"
5) (2) BRASS

d7
SECTION   3"=1'0"

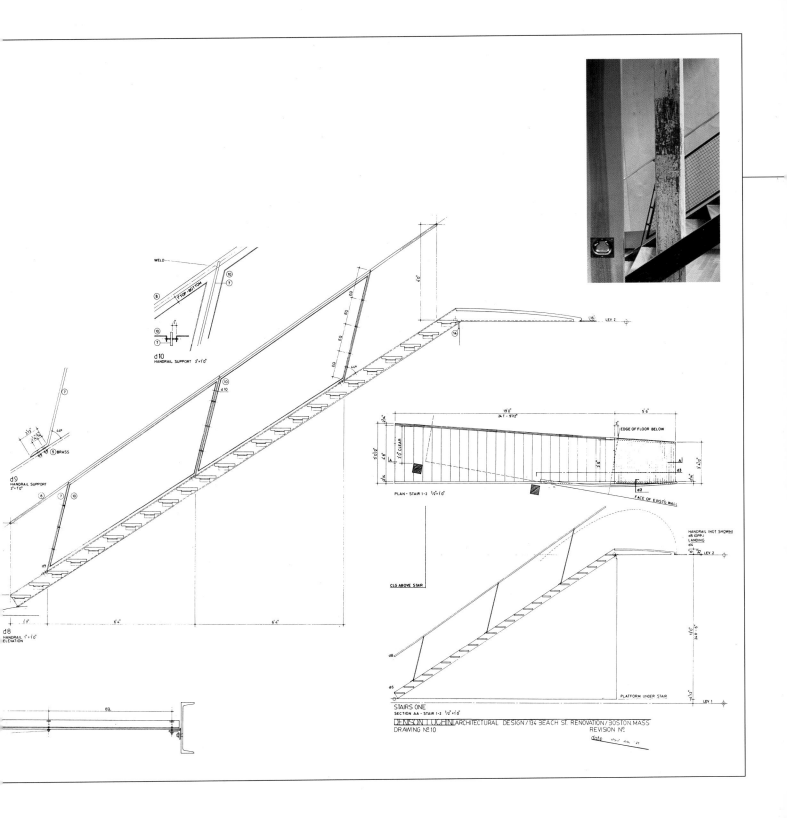

THIRD FLOOR PLAN
1. TERRACE
2. LIBRARY

SECOND FLOOR PLAN
1. BATHROOM
2. DRESSING ROOM
3. BEDROOM
4. SITTING
5. READING
6. STUDY
7. STUDY

FIRST FLOOR PLAN
1. MUSIC
2. SITTING
3. DINING
4. KITCHEN
5. STORAGE
6. MACHINERY
7. BATH
8. LAUNDRY
9. ENTRANCE
10. BAR

The floor plans show how the curved wall in the second floor is clad in copper, conceived as a "tympan" that causes the stairs to reverberate through the three levels of the apartment. This registers in the plan, dictating the position of these elements in space.

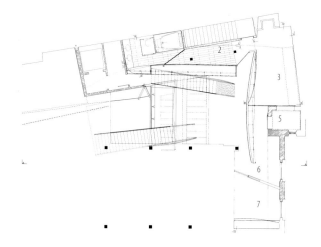

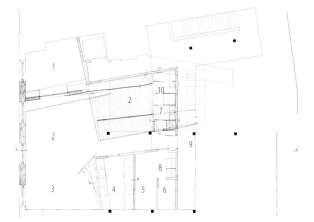

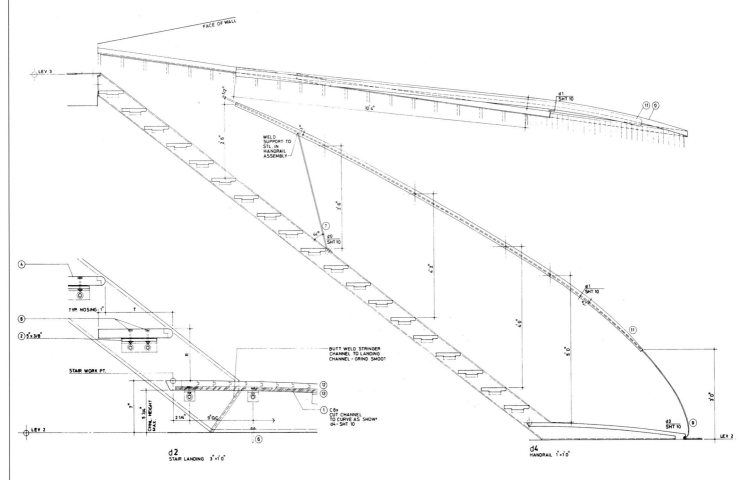

FACE OF WALL

LEV 3

WELD
SUPPORT TO
STL. IN
HANDRAIL
ASSEMBLY

d1
SHT 10

11 9

2'-6"

3'-6"

7

d0
SHT 10

4'-0"

4'-2"

10'-4"

d1
SHT 10

11

4'-9"

5'-0"

3'-0"

d3
SHT 10

9

LEV 2

4

TYP. NOSING 1"   T

6

2 5" x 3/8"

BUTT WELD STRINGER
CHANNEL TO LANDING
CHANNEL - GRIND SMOOT

STAIR WORK PT.

R

12

13

7"

5 3/4"

CHNL. HEIGHT
MAX.

2 1/4"   9" O.C.

1 C 8x
CUT CHANNEL
TO CURVE AS SHOW
d4- SHT 10

LEV 2

6

d2
STAIR LANDING 3"=1'0"

d4
HANDRAIL 1"=1'0"

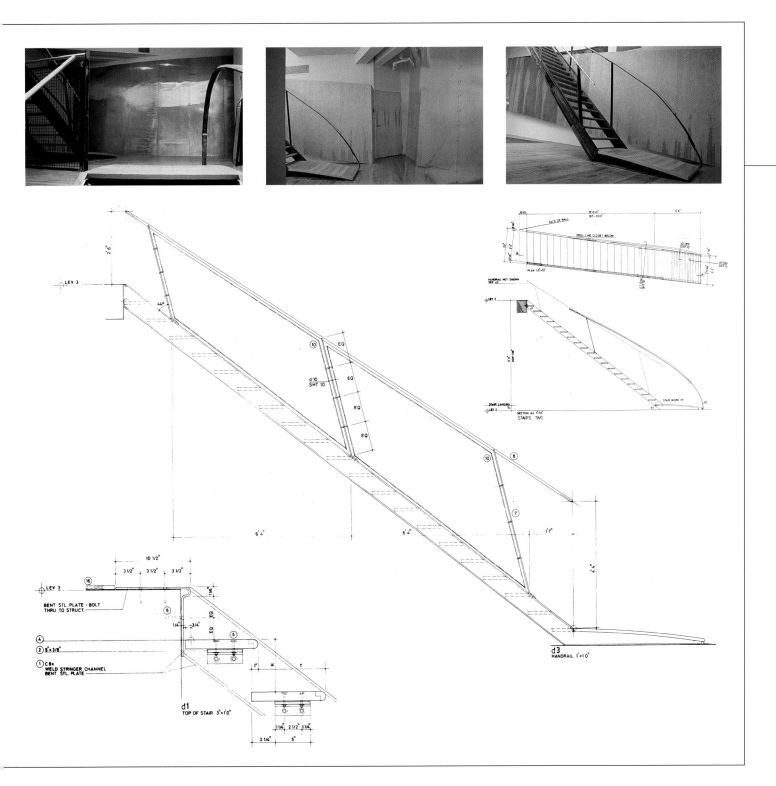

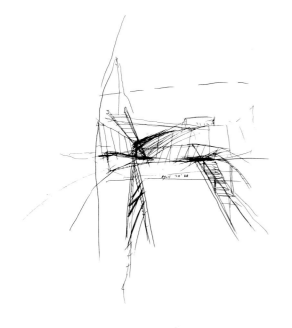

Close-up of the wall dividing the master bedroom from the sitting area, a follow-up to the sketches shown on the next page that show the initial intention to find a curvilinear form and a reflective material to capture the condition of reverberation, like an echo (opposite page).

Heilig Residence

ST. LOUIS, MISSOURI

A line is a long, stretched note. Everything can happen there, from the initiation of a gaze to the echo of a shadow or a sound. When the line is located in a specific place all is registered in its volume, in its density: Objects and happenings are marked with its presence.

This house appears there, in that difficult expectation that demands, perhaps pretentiously, that architecture resides in the ineffable moment when horizon and sky become the same thing . . .
Departing from a program typically found in the mid-size house, this project tries to improve the formal characteristics of the ranch house and produce a stronger relationship with its immediate context. Three outcomes follow:

First, the roof adopts two distinct pitches, an acute one facing the street (and operating as a shield), and a soft one facing the golf course where the best views occur;
second, the typical floor plan orients all tangential walls toward the golf course, which is not perpendicular to the site's edge; and
third, the roof, (and not the plan) becomes the element that registers the distinction between front (street) and back (garden), ground (front) and sky (back), topography (ground) and view (sky), reflection (topography) and transparency (view).

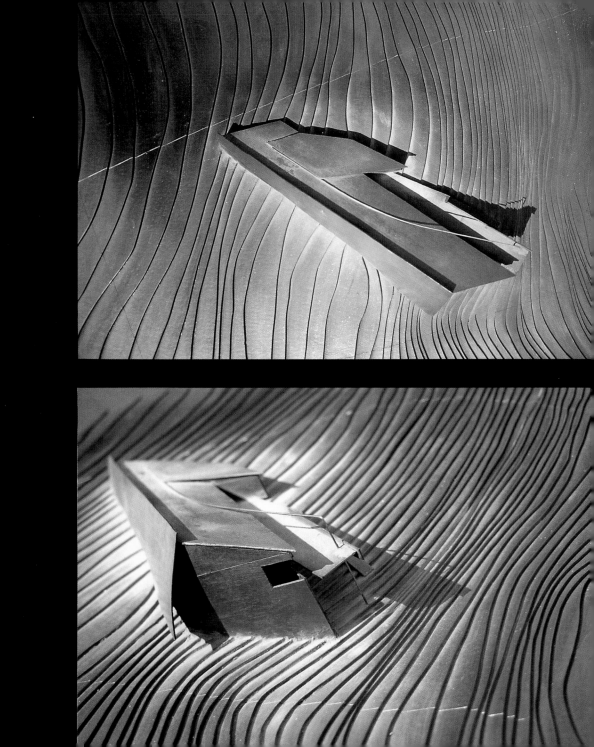

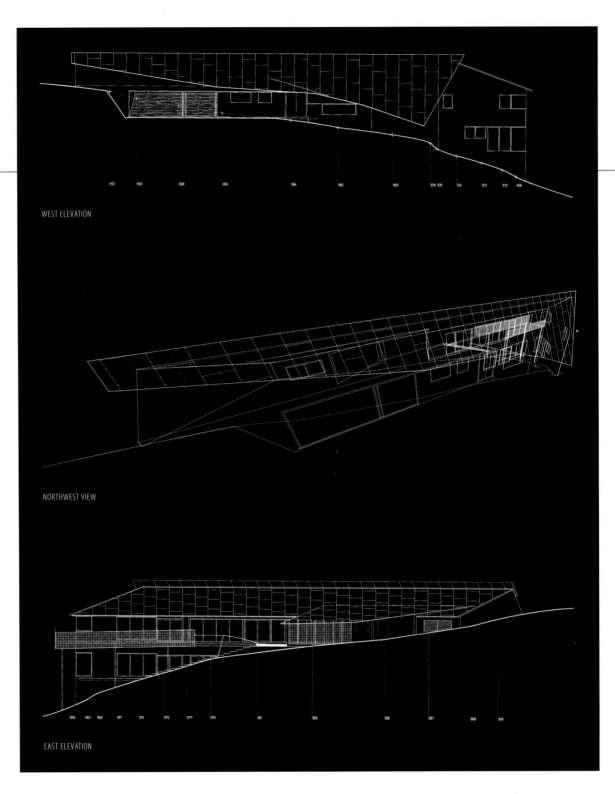

WEST ELEVATION

NORTHWEST VIEW

The roof comprises a double layer of a roofing membrane underneath stainless steel sheets, separated by wood spacers to allow for differences in dilation and breathing. The walls are in white stucco. It was important to utilize two materials (one opaque, one reflective) to capture both the shadows of the existing trees and the changes in the sky.

EAST ELEVATION

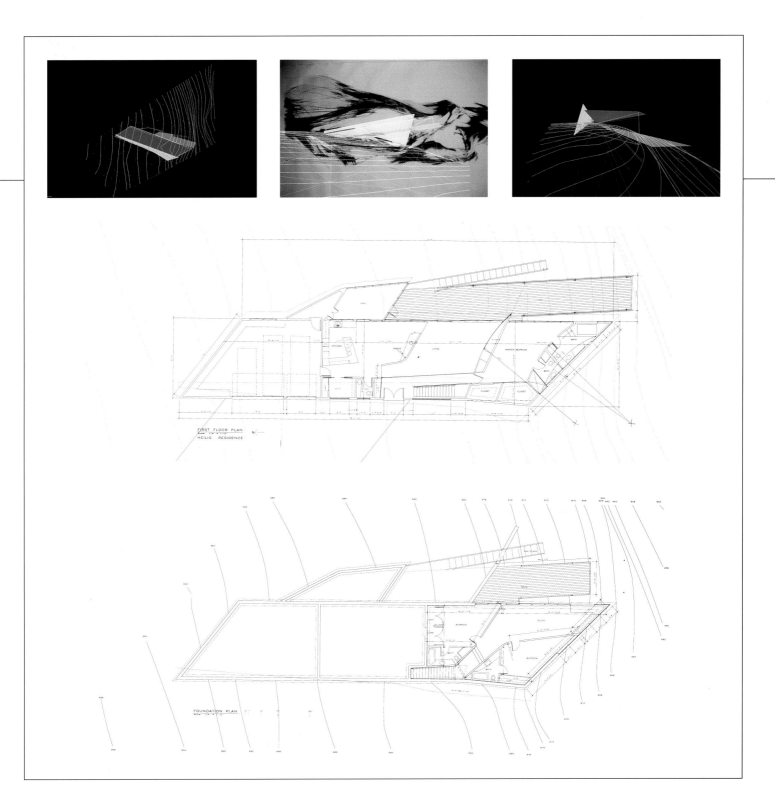

FIRST FLOOR PLAN
HEILIG RESIDENCE

FOUNDATION PLAN

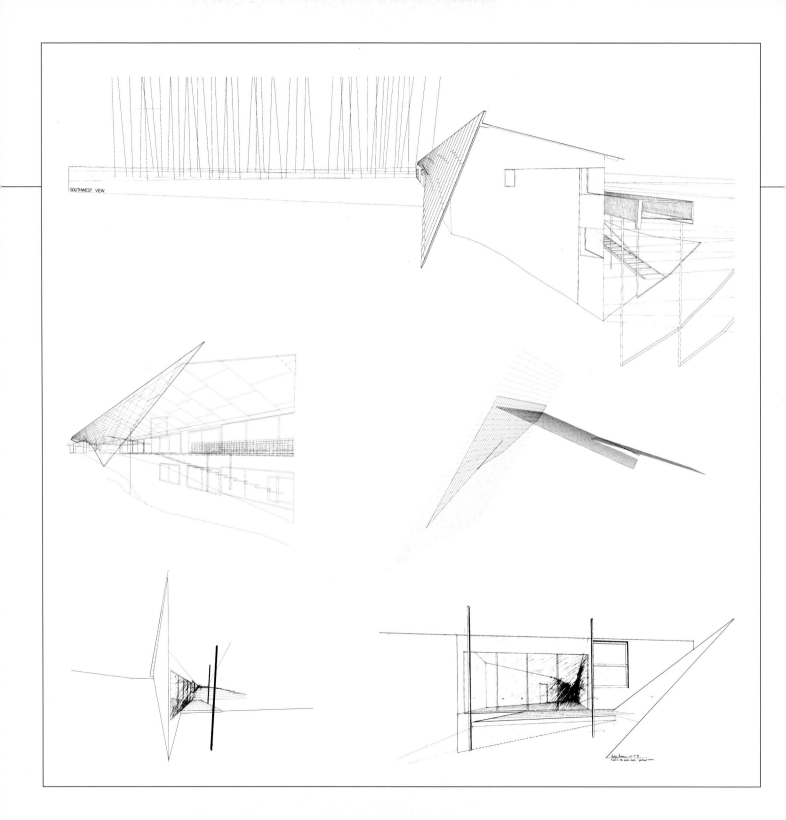

SOUTHWEST VIEW

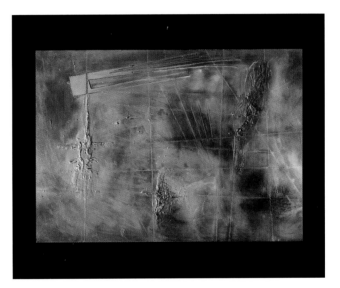

Models and bas-relief study of the concept for the project, understood as the wing of a bird suddenly appearing in the forest, later registering the specific conditions of the topography and the view.

Piku Residence

DETROIT, MICHIGAN   with Dirk Denison

Located in Orchard Lake, Michigan, the half-acre (one-fifth hectare) site is rectangular, with one of its narrow sides touching the lake toward the west. The primary view was one of the main characteristics considered in the siting of the house. The other was the sloping terrain, which drops about nineteen feet (six meters) toward the lake.

It is often understood that the frame controls the perception in the observer and the boundary of the object of perception. This project intends to question that premise by presenting two simultaneous alternatives to the riches of observation: by dividing, folding a single line, the house becomes both an inside space and an exterior object. That is, through the inside we perceive the outside, which is also an interior space. The courtyard appears.

And through it, the landscape unfolds, no longer as an implacable spectacle, but rather as yet another edge. This house is both at the center and marginal to that experience. The observer constantly moves, oscillates in this space of in-between, appropriating simultaneously nature and geometry, landscape and architecture, vision and echo. In short, a true exercise of domestication.

The floor plan is informed by the desire to expose all the rooms of the house towards the lake. The house is thought of as a bar, bent to fit within the width of the site, hence its "V" shape (opposite page).

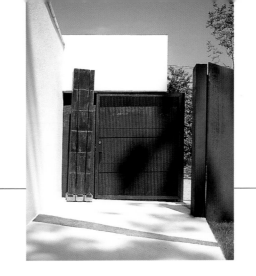

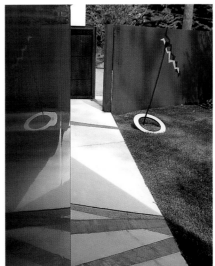

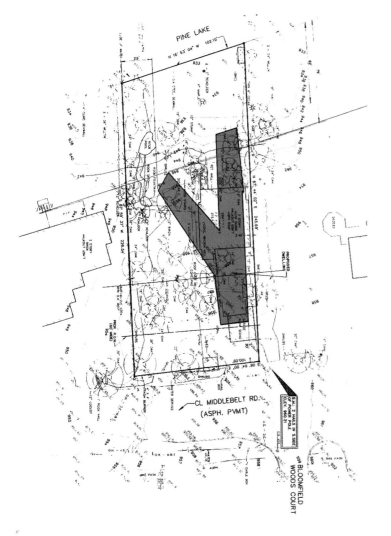

A Cor-Ten steel "band" splits, causing the opening into the site and the house (opposite page). The sequence of openings from the threshold to the entry area in the house (this page).

Initial sketch showing the vortex
caused by the "bending" of the plan,
and photos of the completed project
revealing the in-between space, both
a courtyard (enclosed, delineated)
and a garden (open, limitless).

Piku Residence

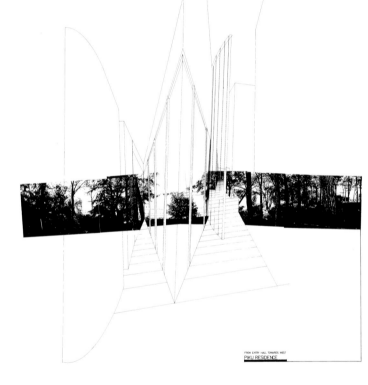

Photos, sketch: The intention is to engage the view-horizon line, or line of sight, the spectacle of the landscape, and the architecture simultaneously—rather than a traditional approach of one "framing" the other. Here both combine to erase differences of foreground/background, inside/outside, natural/man-made.

View from the master bedroom wing looking toward the breakfast area in the living room wing. The proximity of the two walls enhances the complex relation of the two wings, simultaneously showing both the inside and outside of the same space through transparency and reflection.

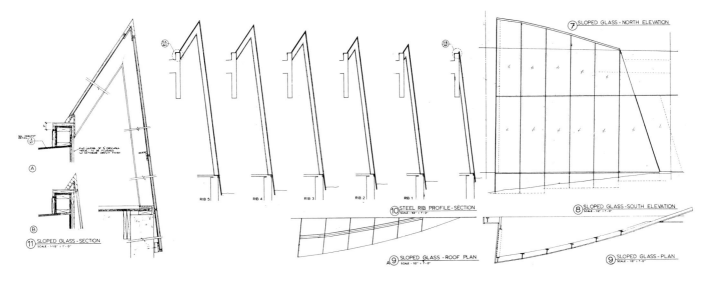

SLOPED GLASS - SECTION
SCALE : 1-1/2" = 1'-0"

RIB 5   RIB 4   RIB 3   RIB 2   RIB 1

STEEL RIB PROFILE - SECTION
SCALE : 1/2" = 1'-0"

SLOPED GLASS - NORTH ELEVATION

SLOPED GLASS - SOUTH ELEVATION
SCALE : 1/2" = 1'-0"

SLOPED GLASS - ROOF PLAN
SCALE : 1/2" = 1'-0"

SLOPED GLASS - PLAN
SCALE : 1/2" = 1'-0"

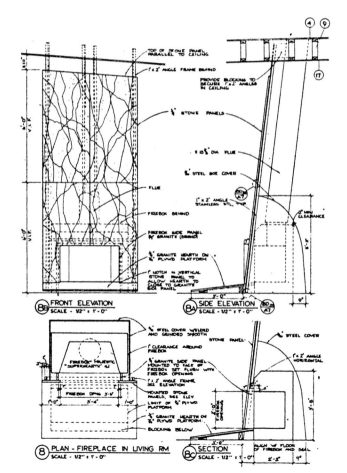

FRONT ELEVATION
SCALE - 1/2" = 1' - 0"

SIDE ELEVATION
SCALE - 1/2" = 1' - 0"

PLAN - FIREPLACE IN LIVING RM
SCALE - 1/2" = 1' - 0"

SECTION
SCALE - 1/2" = 1' - 0"

In the living room, the window opening along the side is split with a frame that endorses the horizon line. This line remains constant, while the volume of the room and the amount of light increase toward the lake, acknowledging the view.

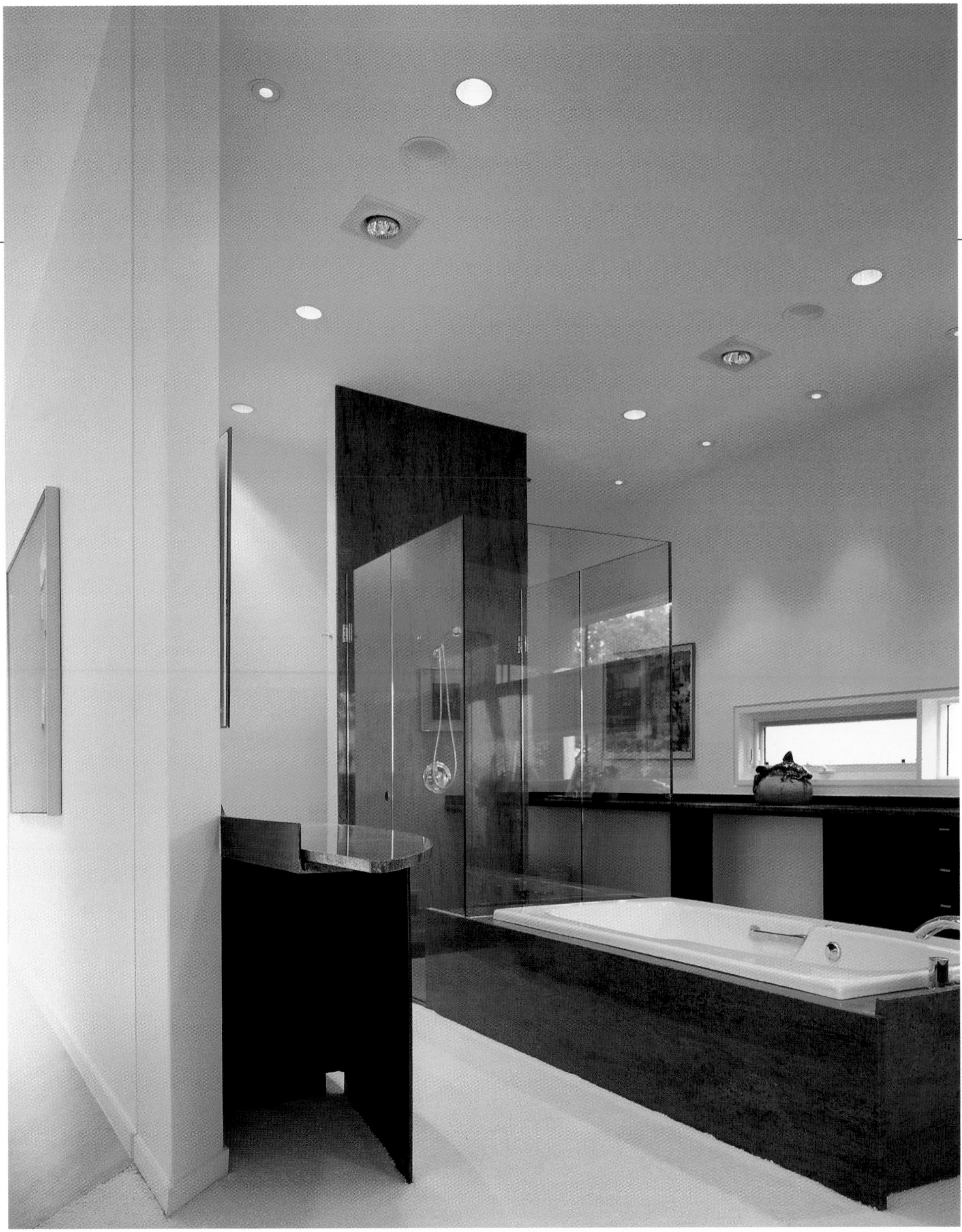

The tub and shower in the master bath divide the space into two areas, yet allow its users to view outside from any position (opposite page). Conversely, in the master bedroom the headboard is exaggerated to be opaque and opposite to the main view. The bed is no longer a piece of furniture; it engages with the architecture of the house.

Maritz-Starek Residence

ST. LOUIS, MISSOURI

Located on Hortense Place, one of the great private streets of St. Louis, the one-acre (half-hectare) site is rectangular, with one of its narrow sides facing the street and the other an alley, while one of its flanks faces Hortense Place, a very busy street. The tall (eight-foot/three-meter) copper-clad concrete fence, plus heavy planting along it, becomes a visual and acoustic barrier against the street.

As an addition and renovation, the project in fact becomes an exercise in avoidance: the old structure, a 1912 mansion located in the Central West End (an historic neighborhood of St. Louis) has strong similarities with the Viennese Secession style. Our proposal involved rebuilding the original columns and cornice (destroyed in 1931), thus bringing back the full sense of monumentality that the mansion originally had. The project also involved the inclusion of a pool, Jacuzzi, garage and deck, along with a new fence surrounding the property and a redesign of the garden, in addition to a complete restoration of the interior spaces, plus the redesign of the kitchen, dining room, master bathroom, guest bathroom, and master bedroom. In this case we opted to establish a very clear distinction between the old and new. Outside, the stairs connecting the sun deck with the deck/Jacuzzi are literally "jumping" over the existing walls, minimizing contact. At the same time, the landing from the stairs becomes a diving platform to the pool, reiterating the intention of avoiding connection to the house. By the same token the new deck stops short of touching the walls of the house, and the new fence (ten feet/three meters high) barely connects with the sun porch on the west side.

The wall at the stairs is built-in stainless steel. The steps and landing are Spanish cedar. The deck is paved with limestone panels. The fence, a ribbon undulating along the property line, is finished with copper sheets.

PROPOSED ADDITIONS
0. EXISTING HOUSE
1. NEW CORNICE
2. COLUMNS
3. COPPER WALL

SOUTH ELEVATION

0
1
2
3

Photos showing the house in its original
condition (1910), in its state prior to
Adrian Luchini's work (1990), and then
after the renovation. The columns and
cornice were reincorporated to enhance
the original sense of solemn scale.

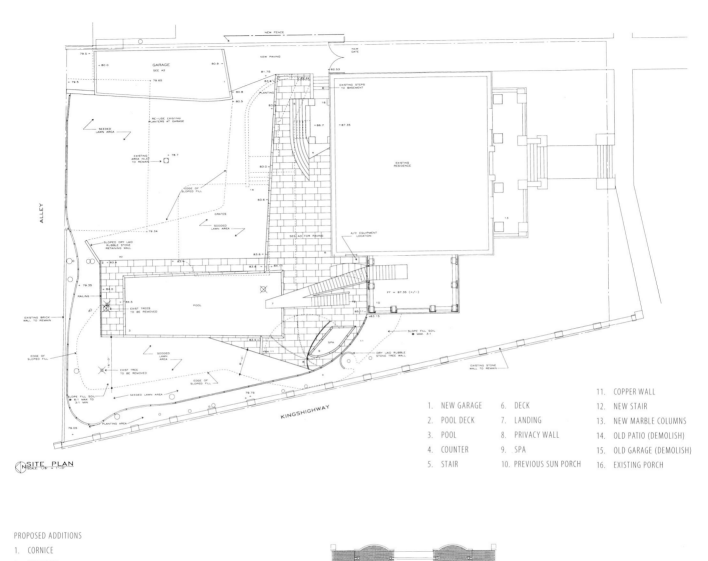

GARAGE
SEE A3

RE-USE EXISTING
PLANTERS AT GARAGE

SEEDED
LAWN AREA

EXISTING
AREA INLET
TO REMAIN

EDGE OF
SLOPED FILL

GRATES

SEEDED
LAWN AREA

SLOPED DRY LAID
RUBBLE STONE
RETAINING WALL

POOL

RAILING

EXISTING BRICK
WALL TO REMAIN

EXIST TREES
TO BE REMOVED

EDGE OF
SLOPED FILL

EXIST TREE
TO BE REMOVED

SODDED
LAWN AREA

EDGE OF
SLOPED FILL

SEEDED LAWN AREA

SLOPE FILL SOIL
@ 6:1 MAX TO
3:1 MIN

PLANTING AREA

NEW FENCE

NEW PAVING

NEW
GATE

EXISTING STEPS
TO BASEMENT

PLANTING

EXISTING
RESIDENCE

A/C EQUIPMENT
LOCATION

SEE A3 FOR PAVING

FF = 87.35 (+/-)

SLOPE FILL SOIL
@ MAX. 3:1

SPA

DRY LAID RUBBLE
STONE TREE WALL

EXISTING STONE
WALL TO REMAIN

KINGSHIGHWAY

ALLEY

SITE PLAN
SCALE 1/8" = 1'-0"

1. NEW GARAGE
2. POOL DECK
3. POOL
4. COUNTER
5. STAIR

6. DECK
7. LANDING
8. PRIVACY WALL
9. SPA
10. PREVIOUS SUN PORCH

11. COPPER WALL
12. NEW STAIR
13. NEW MARBLE COLUMNS
14. OLD PATIO (DEMOLISH)
15. OLD GARAGE (DEMOLISH)
16. EXISTING PORCH

PROPOSED ADDITIONS

1. CORNICE
2. COLUMNS
3. MARBLE STAIR
4. COPPER WALL

KINGS HIGHWAY ELEVATION

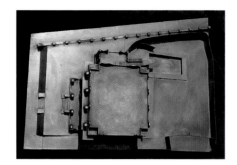

FROM POOL TOWARD SOUTH

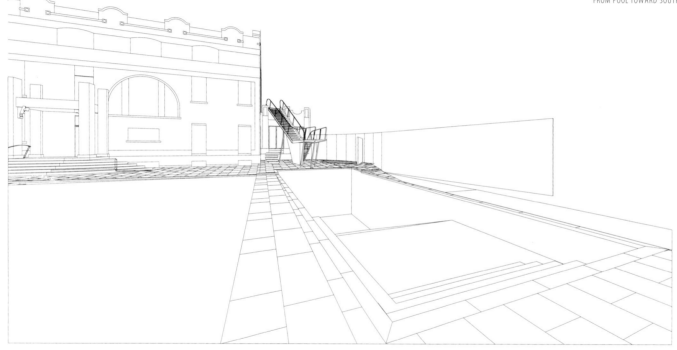

FROM KITCHEN STAIRS

FROM TERRACE TOWARD POOL

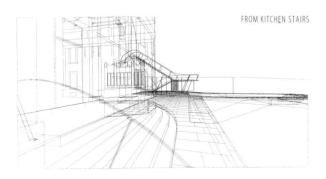

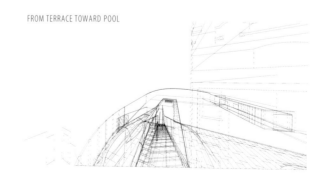

Stainless steel and copper were used for their ability to be both as durable as more traditional materials, such as marble, yet "thin" (conceptually, physically) to avoid a mere mimicking of the existing tectonics of the house.

Maritz-Starek Residence

Details of reflection and light between the copper fence and the pivoting panel that conceals the Jacuzzi when rotated to allow for the privacy of its users. Metal reflection is incorporated as another feature of the garden.

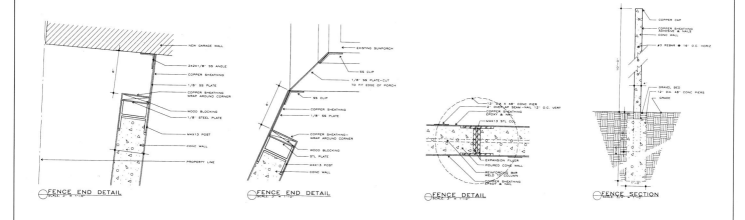

FENCE END DETAIL
SCALE: 3" = 1'-0"

- NEW GARAGE WALL
- 2X2X1/8" SS ANGLE
- COPPER SHEATHING
- 1/8" SS PLATE
- COPPER SHEATHING WRAP AROUND CORNER
- WOOD BLOCKING
- 1/8" STEEL PLATE
- M4X13 POST
- CONC WALL
- PROPERTY LINE

FENCE END DETAIL
SCALE: 3" = 1'-0"

- EXISTING SUNPORCH
- SS CLIP
- 1/8" SS PLATE-CUT TO FIT EDGE OF PORCH
- SS CLIP
- COPPER SHEATHING
- 1/8" SS PLATE
- COPPER SHEATHING-WRAP AROUND CORNER
- WOOD BLOCKING
- STL PLATE
- M4X13 POST
- CONC WALL

FENCE DETAIL
SCALE: 3" = 1'-0"

- 12" DIA X 48" CONC PIER
- 2" OVERLAP SEAM - NAIL 12" O.C. VERT
- COPPER SHEATHING EPOXY & NAIL
- M4X13 STL COL
- EXPANSION FILLER
- POURED CONC WALL
- REINFORCING BAR WELD TO COLUMN
- COPPER SHEATHING EPOXY & NAIL

FENCE SECTION
SCALE: 3/4" = 1'-0"

- COPPER CAP
- COPPER SHEATHING ADHESIVE & NAILS
- CONC WALL
- #3 REBAR @ 16" O.C. HORIZ
- GRAVEL BED
- 12" DIA 48" CONC PIERS
- GRADE

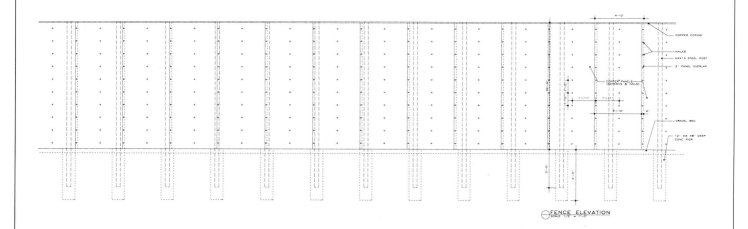

FENCE ELEVATION
SCALE: 1/2" = 1'-0"

- COPPER COPING
- NAILES
- M4X13 STEEL POST
- 2" PANEL OVERLAP
- COPPER PANELS (ADHESIVE & NAILS)
- GRAVEL BED
- 12" DIA 48" DEEP CONC PIER

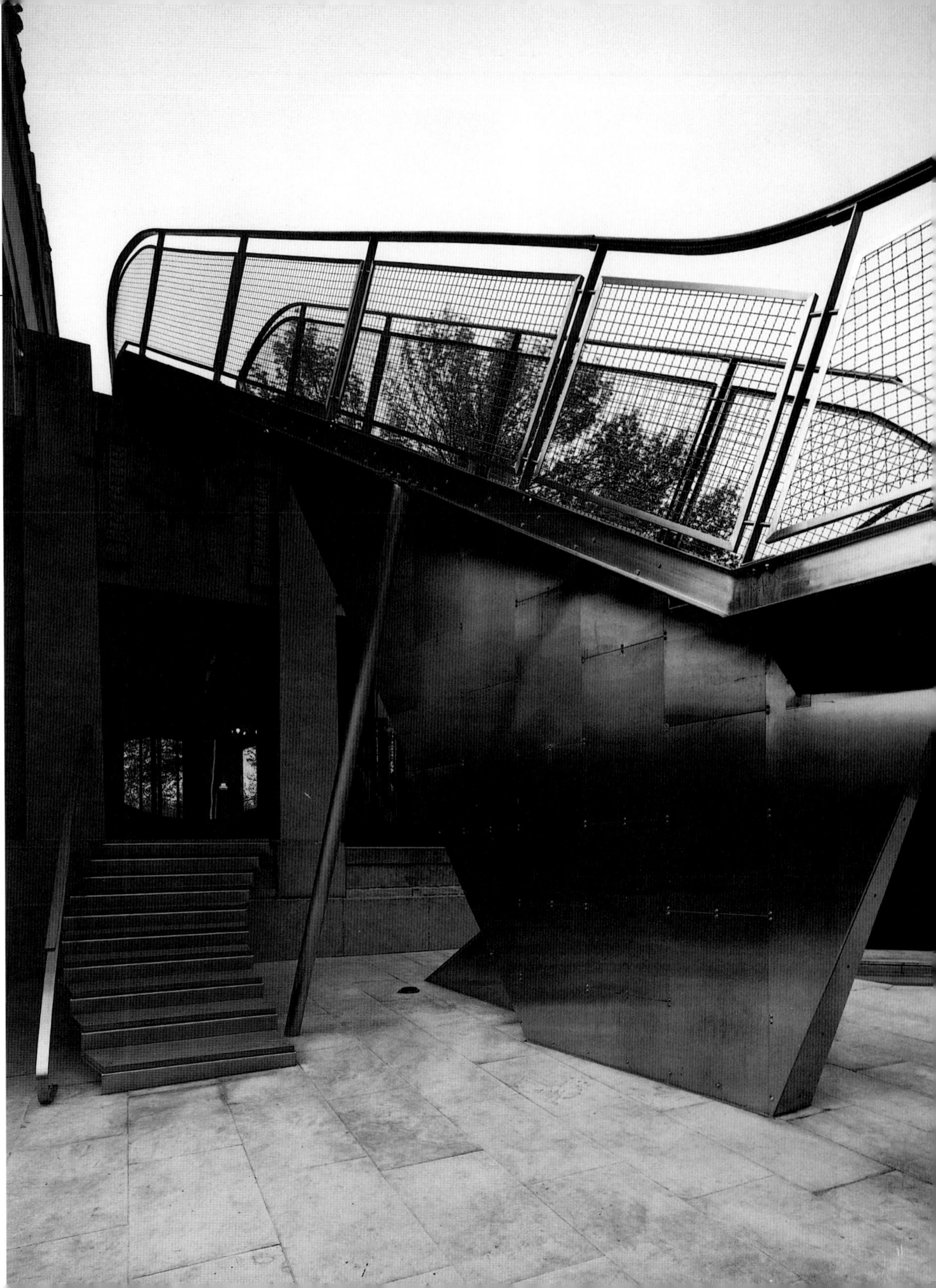

EL SALTO

The stairs descending from the terrace become the occasion to jump into the water—materializing the intention to approach the project by avoiding the need to imitate the existing.

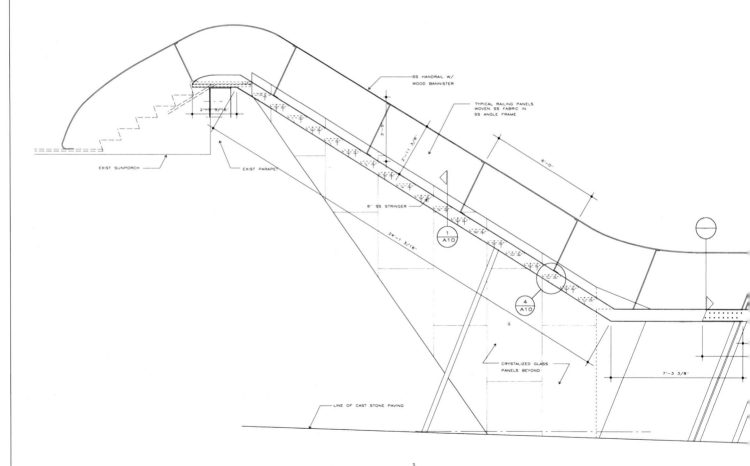

SS HANDRAIL W/
WOOD BANNISTER

TYPICAL RAILING PANELS
WOVEN SS FABRIC IN
SS ANGLE FRAME

EXIST SUNPORCH

EXIST PARAPET

6" SS STRINGER

2'-11 3/16"

6'-0"

24'-1 3/16"

1
A10

4
A10

7'-3 3/8"

CRYSTALIZED GLASS
PANELS BEYOND

LINE OF CAST STONE PAVING

1
AB
EAST STRINGER ELEVATION

SCALE: 1/2" = 1'-0"

END RAILING

END RAILING

3'-0"

TYPICAL RAILING PANEL
W/ SS WOVEN METAL
FABRIC W/ SS ANGLE FRAME

EAST WING BEYOND

3'-0"

TYPICAL RAILING PANEL
W/ SS WOVEN METAL
FABRIC W/ SS ANGLE FRAME

TAPERED 6" SS CHANEL

3/4"

7'-10 1/4"

6'-0 3/4"

2'-2 1/2"

8'-3 1/4"

3 1/2" DIA SS COL (TYP)

SS COLUMNS (TYP)

LINE OF CAST STONE PAVING

CRYSTALIZED
GLASS PANELS

14'-3"

② WEST STRINGER ELEVATION
AB SCALE: 1/2" = 1'-0"

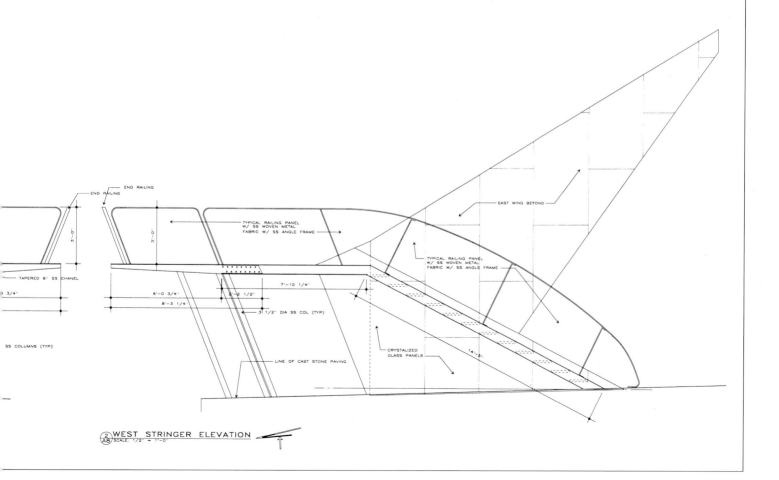

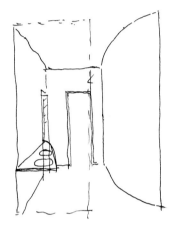

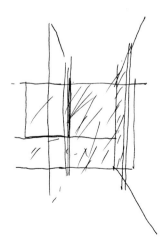

In the master bathroom, frosted, transparent, and reflective glass aid in dematerializing the narrow space and also conceal its function as a bathroom.

Hematian Residence

Located on a waterfront site facing Manhattan and Long Island Sound, the house is organized so that most rooms face the view, while most of the circulation faces the opposite way, toward the entrance.

Considering the large scale of the house and the prevailing views, the massing articulates the two main floors to make the volume seem smaller while maintaining a continuous, fluid form suggesting the continuity of space inside. There is an interaction between the vertical planes of the walls, understood as "liquid" and oscillating, increasing and decreasing in size to provide various openings, and the horizontal plane of the roof, covering also the east side to insure privacy and block unwanted vistas toward the neighbor. The "wavy" character of the result is obviously related to the proximity of the water.

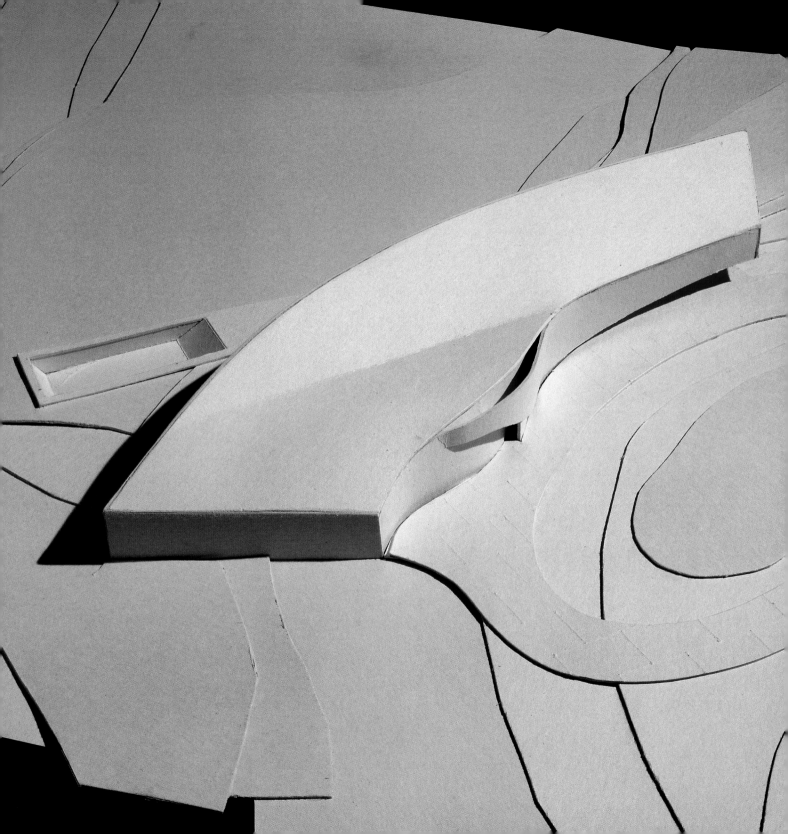

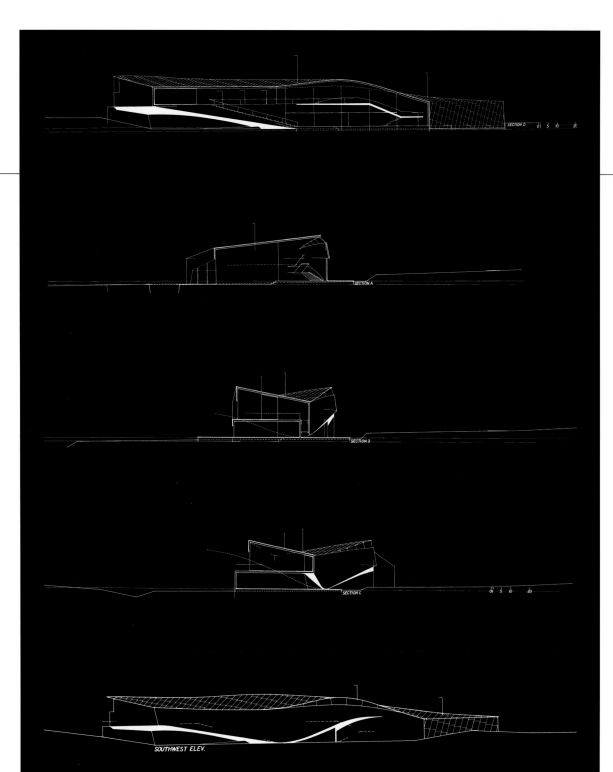

The different spaces of the house as well as the exterior form show a fluidity that echoes the presence of the water at the site, like a fragment of constant motion.

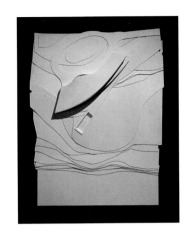

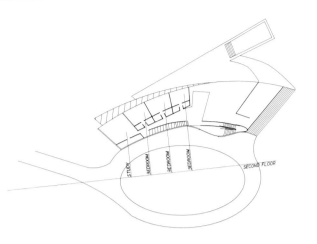

STUDY BEDROOM BEDROOM BEDROOM   SECOND FLOOR

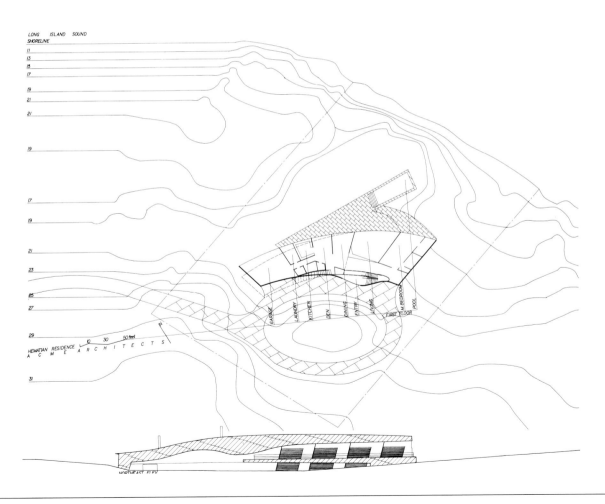

LONG ISLAND SOUND
SHORELINE

11
13
15
17
19
21
21

19

17
19

21
23
25
27

29

HEMATIAN RESIDENCE   10   30   50 feet
A C M E   A R C H I T E C T S

31

GARAGE LAUNDRY KITCHEN DEN DINING ENTRY LOUNGE M. BEDROOM POOL   FIRST FLOOR

NORTHEAST ELEV.

Camp Beersheba Chapel

BEERSHEBA SPRINGS, TENNESSEE

As a part of a complex of cabins and dormitories, this chapel sits in a prominent location on a United Methodist summer camp. This is a wooded site with bungalows and dormitories.

Conceptually, the project is conceived as two large hands (the roof) hosting and protecting the user from the array of activities happening around. Careful consideration was given to the distribution of natural light and sound insulation. The roof, held from the interior by means of exposed trusses, gradually tilts upwards toward the altar, and it is separated from the ground by a continuous glass wall. This creates the illusion of the roof "levitating," while carefully framing the exterior views along the nave. Only at the altar is the user able to look up the sky through the full height of the glass wall behind it.

By carefully controlling the amount of light into the nave, a sense of privacy is created while maintaining a strong connection with the surroundings. The nave of the building is oriented toward an existing outdoor cross.

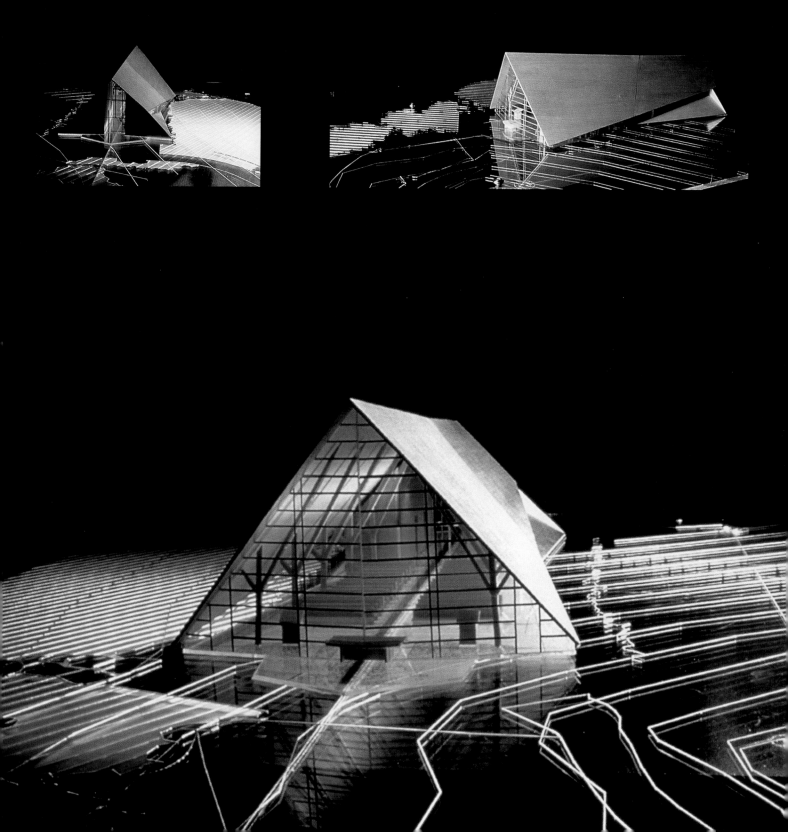

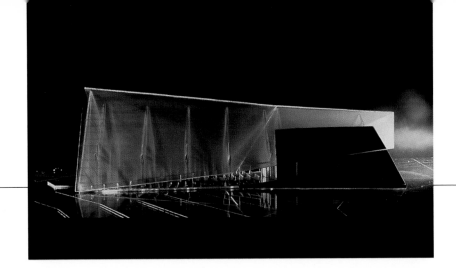

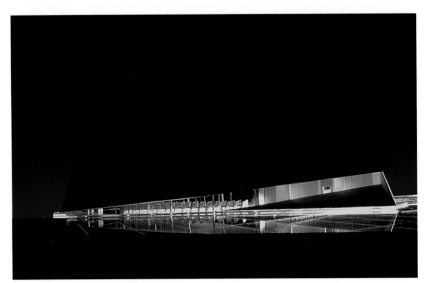

Plan, sections: the shape grows toward the altar. This gesture is used both in plan and in section to increase the sense of drama inside the chapel. The glass surface aids in disengaging the walls from the roof to better express the intention of making it float above the nave (opposite page).

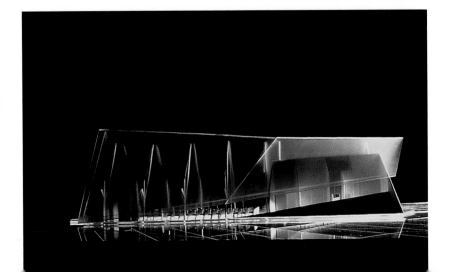

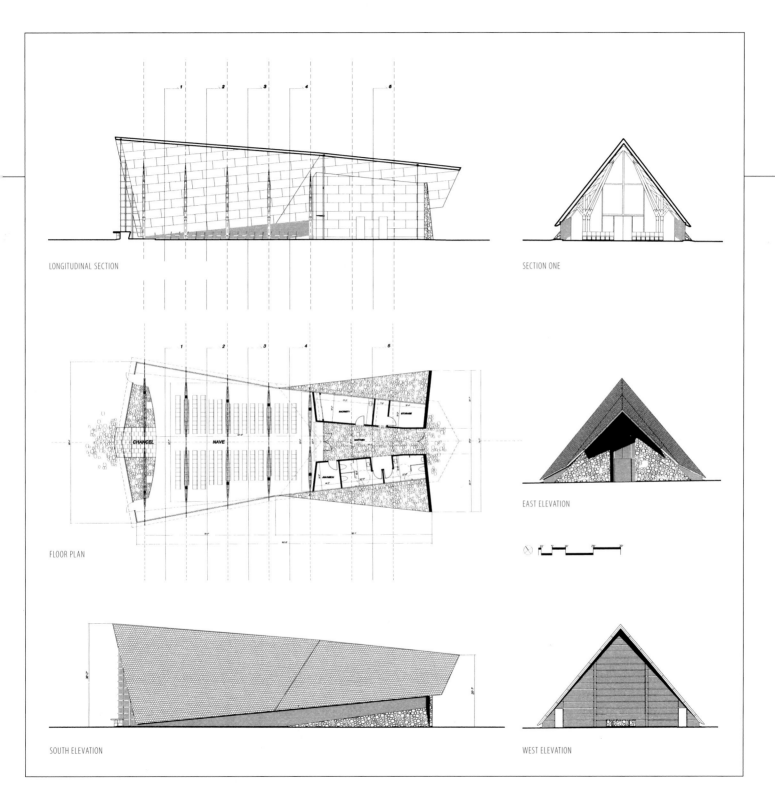

LONGITUDINAL SECTION

SECTION ONE

FLOOR PLAN

CHANCEL   NAVE

EAST ELEVATION

SOUTH ELEVATION

WEST ELEVATION

Camp Beersheba Chapel

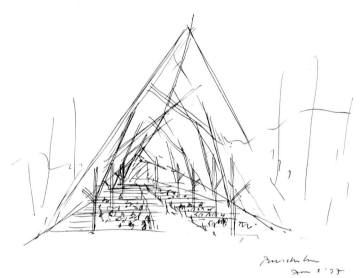

Sketch: from the outset, the church was
thought as a roof or a shadow claiming
a space where prayer would be possible.
The strong formal shape intends to
reflect the simple yet powerful architecture of the bungalows nearby.

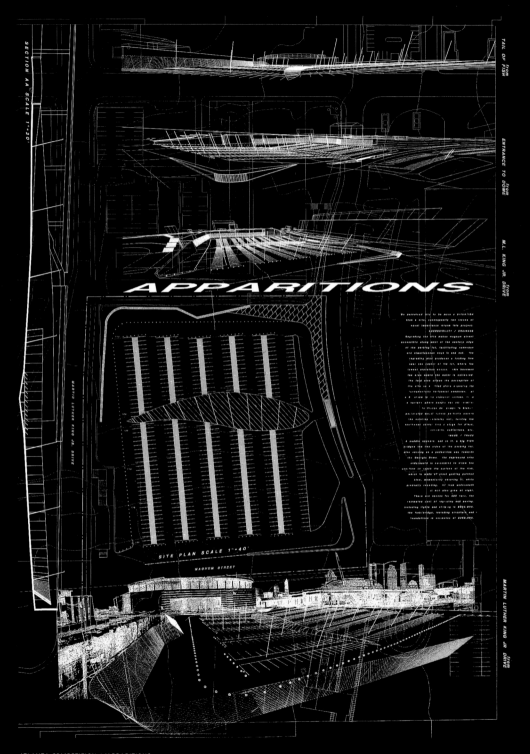

APPARITIONS

Loose Words, Gestures ▶

Not unlike a weaving operation, simultaneously aligning intentions with images, disparate territories with recognizable names, intricate identities with precise profiles, synthesis. In this case, hypotheses of understanding result from considering several issues at the same time, when the dialogue with the client and the site are an integral part of the process of design, and when it is imperative to acknowledge this condition as instrumental for the development of the project. An oscillation.

The Arms of Manhattan

This project intends to investigate the possibility of disfiguration and its implication in architectural design. Part of the design process was conducted with the aid of a computer that was programmed to draw perspectives as a means of representation of architectural space. In this regard, the task was to incorporate the computer during the development of the idea, that is, to use the computer as a research tool whose capability would allow it to make further decisions rather than using it as a mere instrument of depiction.

The project begins with the proposition of a series of ramps that connect the Manhattan network of streets to the piers adjacent to the edge of the island, looking at the Hudson River. Once the initial ramps (called Ramps "A") were situated, the computer was able to intervene. It was asked, specifically, to draw the ramps from 90 feet below ground, thus having to do with the fact that Manhattan as a network can be "read" from ground level or from above, but never from below. Here the intention was to offer a momentary view of the city thus far denied to the observer, i.e., from below ground. After the computer drawing, the perspectively disfigured ramp was brought to the surface and re-accommodated according to the former position. In order to make clear that the ramp was there previously, it became necessary to maintain both ramps at once, this second one called "Ramp B". At this point there was a conflict; the computer could not treat Ramp B as another ramp; it was still understood as a representation of Ramp A. This is to say, it had no presence as a plan-notation. The plan of Ramp B, therefore, had to be deduced from the initial deformation of Ramp A. After the plan was defined, it was grafted in the site by the plan of Ramp A. Now the plan of Ramp B became a perspectival deformation of Ramp A as it stood from below. From the plan of Ramp B, further work was done in order to obtain sectional information, again derived from the perspectival representation of Ramp A and its sectional condition. Once this was done, the computer was asked again to draw a perspective, now of Ramps A and B.

The process could carry on, but it was suspended at this moment, when the representation of the first artifact— Ramp A—was registered and noted as another artifact, Ramp B, which became no longer just a representation but an object able to be represented as well. The observer, fundamental component within the perspectival perception, is simultaneously offered two alternatives of the same object, now split in two versions which disarm the authority of a privileged point of view since there are at least two; furthermore, the observer is simultaneously able to read both ramps and thus form a new perspectival illusion, or realize that at the same time he or she has become also a disfigured observer, both occupying the privileged point of origin (of vision) and at the same time being (observed) from below in the act of observation.

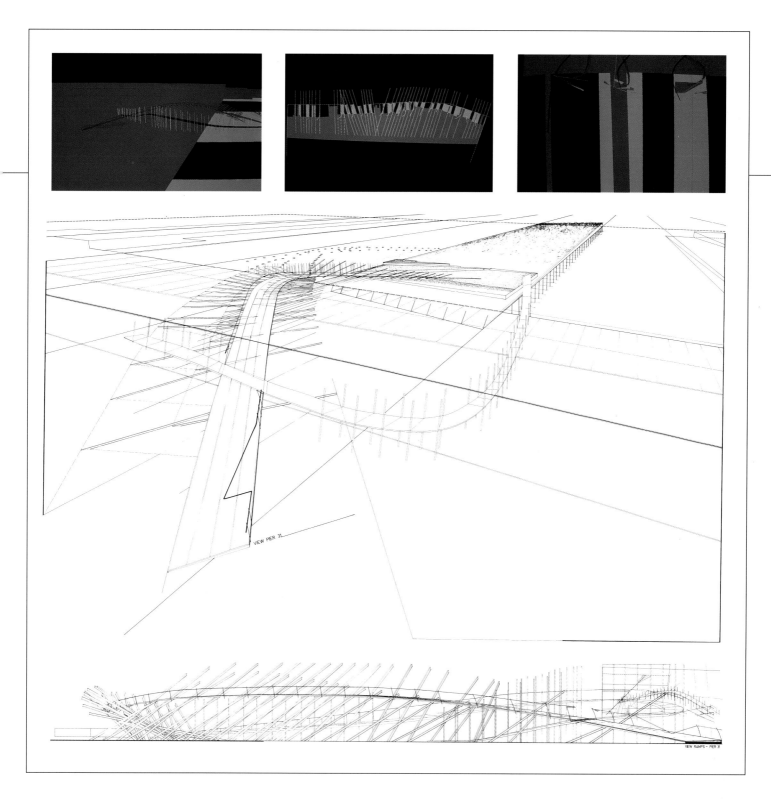

VIEW PIER 31

VIEW RAMPS - PIER 31

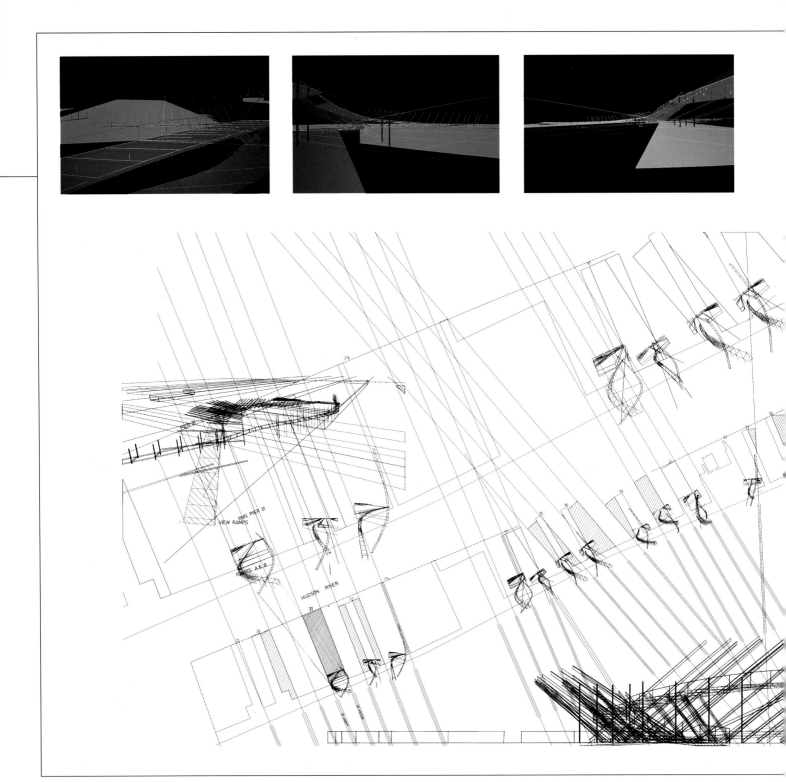

RMS PIER 31
VIEW RAMPS

RAMPS A & B

HUDSON RIVER

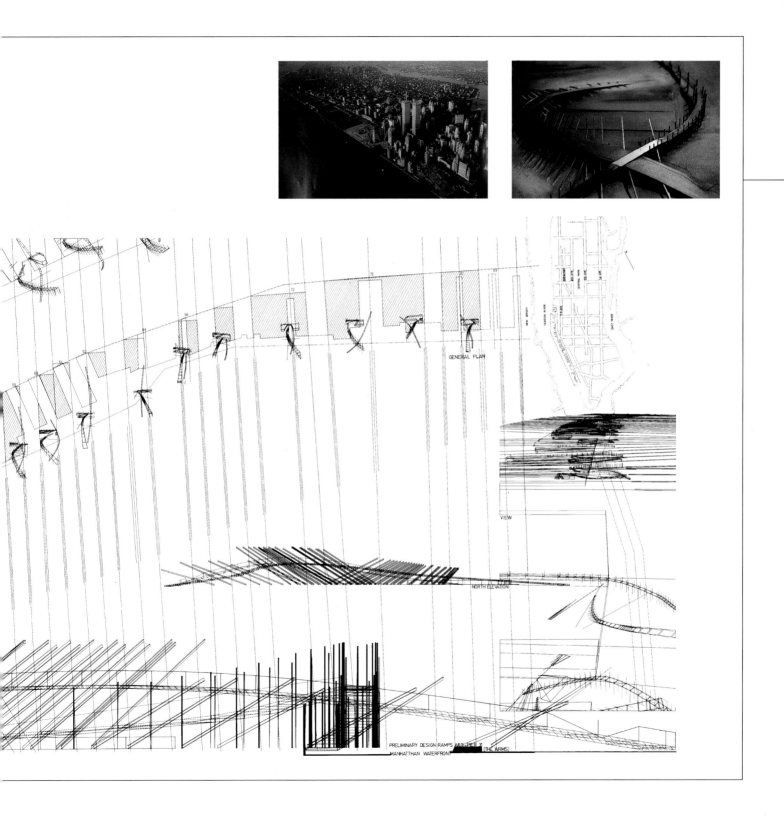

GENERAL PLAN

VIEW

NORTH ELEVATION

PRELIMINARY DESIGN RAMPS AND PIER 3 [THE ARMS]
MANHATTHAN WATERFRONT

KDNL-TV/The Fox

ST. LOUIS, MISSOURI

To attempt a description of the work done at KDNL is an exercise in contradiction. As a series of discrete interventions restricted by the pressure of too large a program within the boundaries of an existing building, this project attempts to neutralize the space by rendering it as a background. And in this withdrawal, the walls within it remain as empty signs, voiceless and nameless, without a physical image. Light, on the other hand, is allowed to invest the different areas with different characters, by changing in intensity and color as it organizes the spaces to work (cold) or circulate (warm).

The work areas are organized in such a way that they submit to the natural flow of circulation and the character of the space available. Despite the intricacy of the program, it was intended to create a fluid space opening longitudinal views and yielding a sense of expanse and continuity. A previously unused hallway was filled with light; a tilted wall creates the illusion of being either longer or shorter than its actual length, depending on the side from which it is approached.

A fundamentally neutral color scheme—sought to maximize flexibility of use—is accentuated by combining cold and warm light sources.

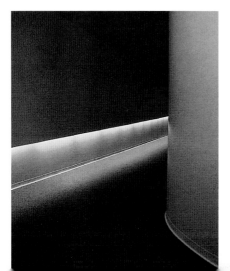

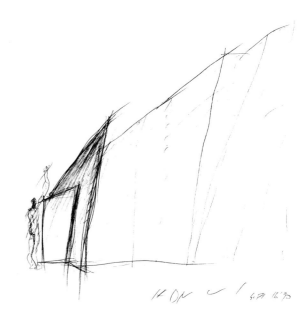

The specific use of light and the
arrangement of light fixtures
qualify the circulation spaces.
This also enriches these spaces
beyond their utilitarian need
while serving their purpose.

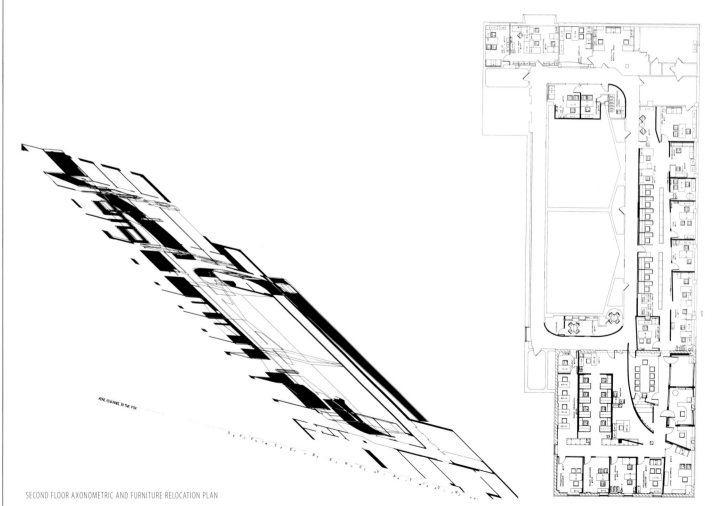

SECOND FLOOR AXONOMETRIC AND FURNITURE RELOCATION PLAN

Sixth Church of Christ, Scientist

Close your hands, and don't move.
Pray,
or meditate,

or establish the circumstances that mark the limits of your territory, momentarily isolating you from the world:
Arrange, in other words, the margins that allow you to say "here" and "now" … This project is (precisely) an effort
to fabricate a single point. What follows is a white echo made of the familiar: names, materials, code, gravity, money.
As a renovation to an existing corner shop, the main challenge was to change the image of the building from an
utilitarian to a religious use. By adding two large, white, out-of-scale walls at the corner intersection, the entrance
is rearranged and part of the existing façade is covered. This double gesture of erasure and construction gives the
new character to the building. Inside, a diagonal intersects the shell and accommodates the various parts of the program,
leaving one large area for the reading room and entry hall, and several small rooms for reading, day school, nursery,
and offices. Between them all services are placed (bathrooms, mechanical rooms, closets).

Due to the limited budget, a single material (drywall) and a single color (celestial white) is used throughout, minimizing
labor cost. Outside the white walls leave two distinct openings: one vertical, for the access of people, the other
horizontal, for the display of books along the major road.

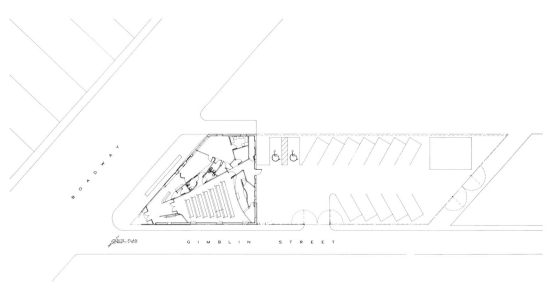

Photos showing the two large exterior walls that create the main opening into the church. At night this opening allows for much light to come out, literally a hole filled with light.

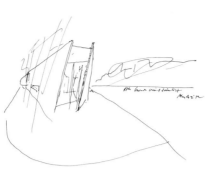

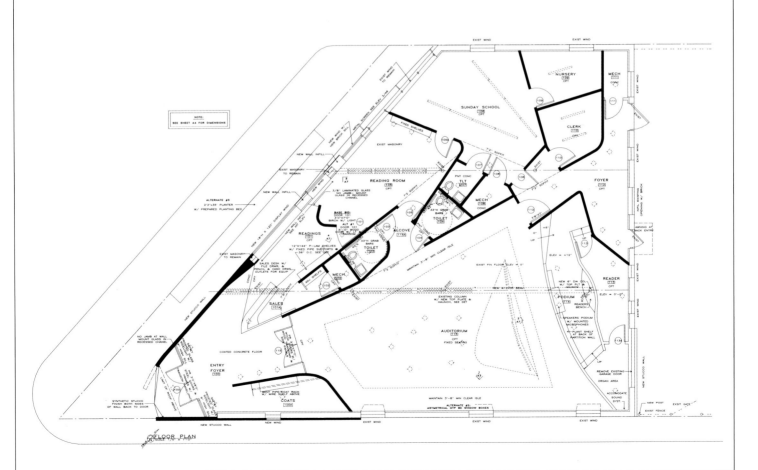

FLOOR PLAN

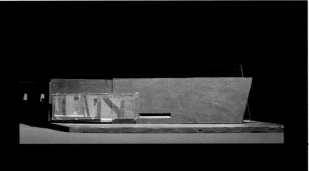

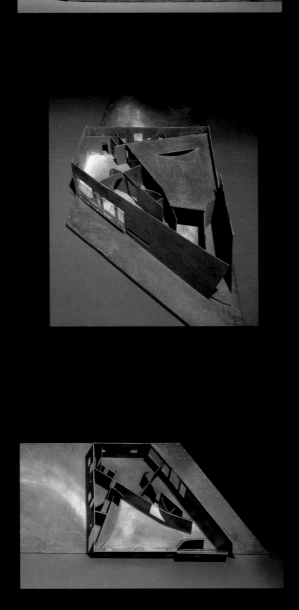

Model showing three basic walls organizing the layout of the project: two exterior walls complete the corner and produce the main opening-entry, and the diagonal at the center of the existing space establishes boundaries for the reading room and offices/reception areas.

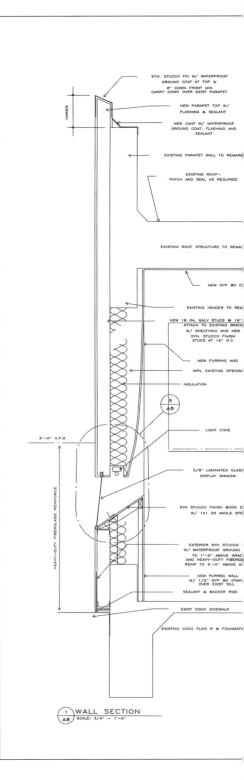

SYN. STUCCO FIN W/ WATERPROOF
GROUND COAT AT TOP &
6" DOWN FRONT MIN
CARRY DOWN OVER EXIST PARAPET

NEW PARAPET TOP W/
FLASHING & SEALANT

NEW CANT W/ WATERPROOF
GROUND COAT, FLASHING AND
SEALANT

EXISTING PARAPET WALL TO REMAIN

EXISTING ROOF—
PATCH AND SEAL AS REQUIRED

VARIES

EXISTING ROOF STRUCTURE TO REMA

NEW GYP BD C

EXISTING HEADER TO REM

NEW 18 GA, GALV STUDS @ 16"
ATTACH TO EXISTING BRICK
W/ SHEATHING AND NEW
SYN. STUCCO FINISH
STUDS AT 16" O.C.

NEW FURRING AND

INFIL EXISTING OPENIN

INSULATION

5
A8

LIGHT COVE

5'-0" A.F.G.

3/8" LAMINATED GLAS
DISPLAY WINDOW

HEAVY-DUTY FIBERGLASS REINFORCE

SYN STUCCO FINISH BOOK D
W/ 1X1 SS ANGLE STO

EXTERIOR SYN STUCCO
W/ WATERPROOF GROUND
TO 1'-0" ABOVE GRAD
AND HEAVY-DUTY FIBERGE
REINF TO 5'-0" ABOVE G

NEW FURRED WALL
W/ 1/2" GYP BD (PAIN
OVER EXIST SILL

SEALANT & BACKER ROD

EXIST CONC SIDEWALK

EXISTING CONC FLOO R & FOUNDATI

1
A8
WALL SECTION
SCALE: 3/4" = 1'-0"

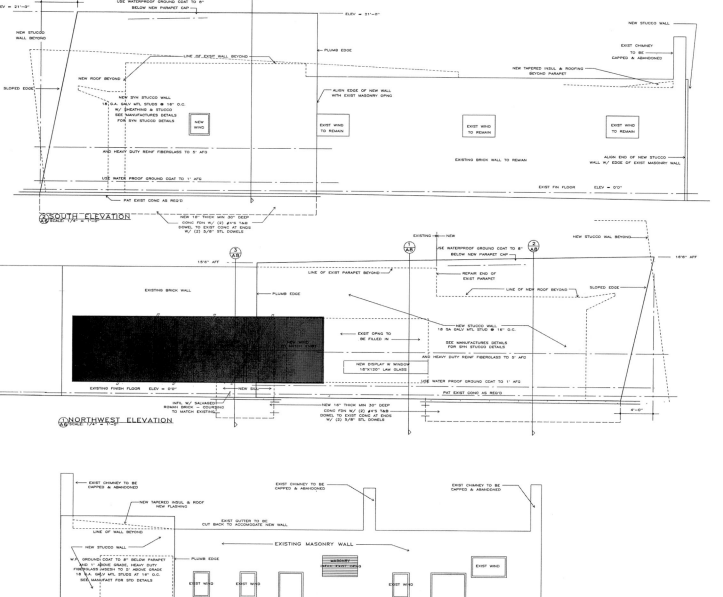

② SOUTH ELEVATION
A6 SCALE: 1/4" = 1'-0"

① NORTHWEST ELEVATION
A6 SCALE: 1/4" = 1'-0"

④ EAST ELEVATION
A6 SCALE: 1/4" = 1'-0"

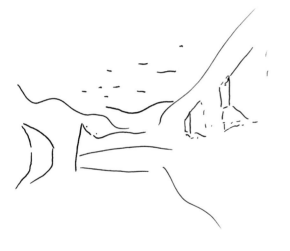

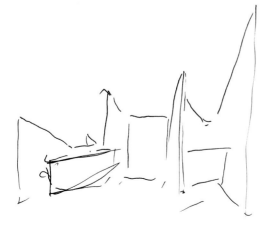

A view of the folded drywall partition allowing space for the window display of books and the outside penetration of light into the reception area (opposite page).

Koplar Residence

Located on the coast of Oregon with the spectacular views of the Pacific Ocean, the house sits in the property with the clear intention to maximize the relationship of the interior spaces with the west view. The house is very open toward the ocean and at the same time quite closed to the street. Since the road into the property slopes toward the west, at street level the roof is the main "façade."

... Like speaking too quickly, break the ranch: a broken line, too much horizon, not to say anything about the wind, or the only way to move the vanishing point out into the horizon and fabricate a sound out of it. This is probably closer: the fabrication, and subsequent disguise of a breaking sound, so persistent in the site.

The fundamental issue was to establish full contact with the site. Inside, the house is divided in two wings, south and north, and the plan has two levels. The lower level is dedicated to public activities such as dining and living, as well as the children's quarters. The upper level contains the a guest bedroom and sitting area (south wing) and exercise room, sauna, and master bedroom suite. Both wings are connected by a double-height space used for dining and meeting. It is also an atrium with a large skylight extending the full width of the house.

A view of the entry/reception area showing the meeting of the two roofs of the house becoming a skylight (above). A view of the master bedroom at the end of the north wing (below).

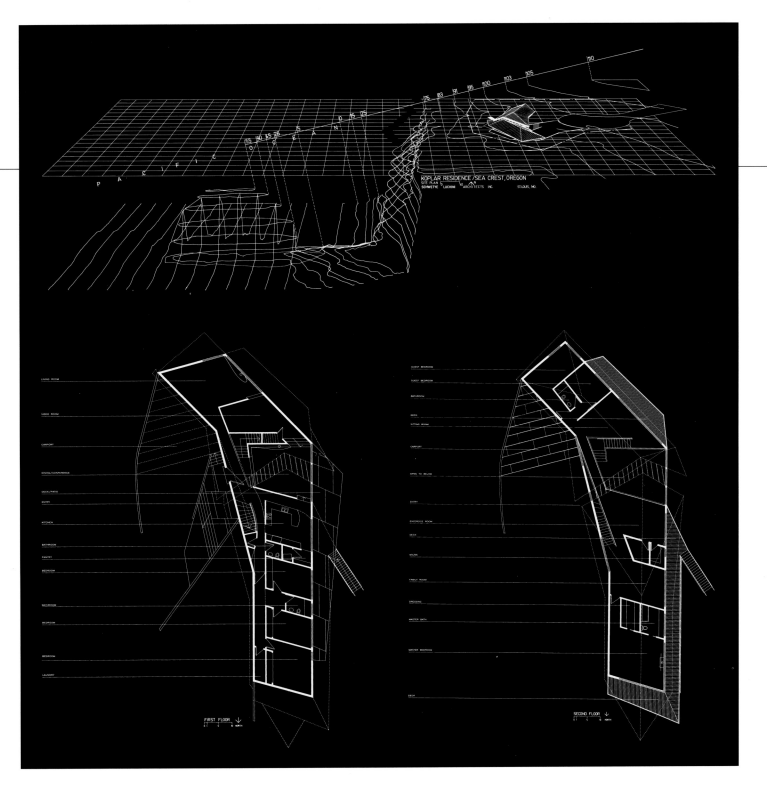

KOPLAR RESIDENCE / SEA CREST, OREGON
SITE PLAN
SCHWETYE LUCHINI ARCHITECTS INC.   ST. LOUIS, MO.

PACIFIC OCEAN

LIVING ROOM
VIDEO ROOM
CARPORT
DINING/CONFERENCE
DECK/PATIO
ENTRY
KITCHEN
BATHROOM
PANTRY
BEDROOM
BATHROOM
BEDROOM
BEDROOM
LAUNDRY

FIRST FLOOR   NORTH

GUEST BEDROOM
GUEST BEDROOM
BATHROOM
DECK
SITTING ROOM
CARPORT
OPEN TO BELOW
ENTRY
EXERCISE ROOM
DECK
SAUNA
FAMILY ROOM
DRESSING
MASTER BATH
MASTER BEDROOM
DECK

SECOND FLOOR   NORTH

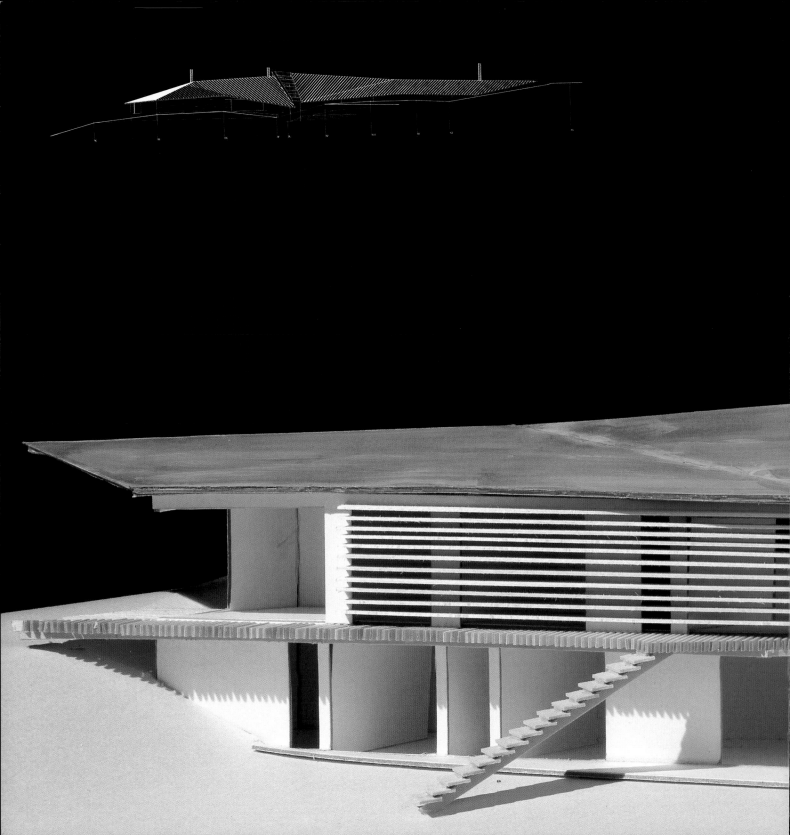

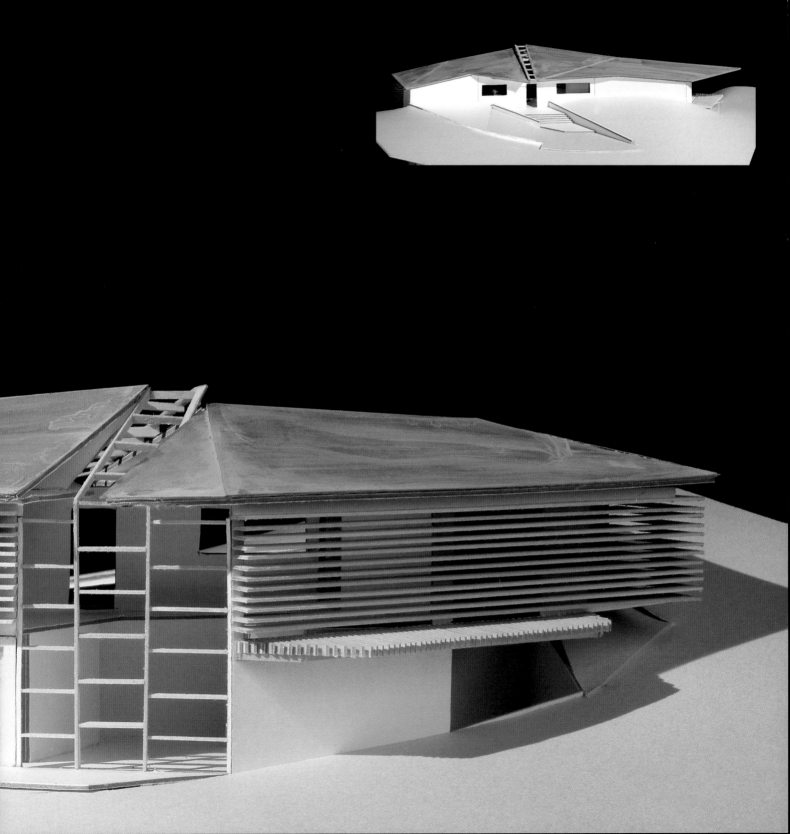

Atlanta Competition

Site 1: Encompassing an area of about seven acres (three hectares), the challenge was to offer suggestions to improve the corridor where a highway runs eighteen feet (six meters) below grade.

(Topiary) . . .to enable a single gesture, a single operation, to encompass all aspects of the project, all possible scales, all moments: it has to be an imprecise gesture, a figure or a scene. A topiary is proposed. Conceived as a tensile structure covered by stressed wire mesh, it extends over the existing gap, performing both as an artificial topography and an event. Depending on the angle of observation, the mesh willappear solid or transparent. It will remain still and quiet, or move and whisper according to the wind, and its shadow will be cast on the highway surface, constantly running away from the course of the sun.

From below it discloses fragments of the sky, from above it is a red patch, and at ground level it is a landscape that turns solid as it touches the street intersections. Here the topiary is a berm made of light metal structure and fiberglass, and it glows at night.

Site 2 (see page 72): Located next to the Georgia Dome, the site was used as surface parking below the street grade, with a single entry/egress point through a ramp. A major drain pipe exists in the center of the lot, and it can't be moved. (Apparitions) Rather than proposing a new use for the site, we opted to redesign the parking arrangement, perceiving this case to be more a situation than a site. Consequently, two issues of importance inform the project:

Accessibility and drainage: By regrading the site along its eastern edge, numerous points of access to the parking area are possible, while a folding line occurs at the center of the lot, where the lowest elevation occurs. Here is where the water will be collected.

Image/trace: A puddle appears, and on it a big fish bridges the two sides of the parking lot, a pedestrian bridge leading toward the stadium entrances. The depressed area underneath is calculated to allow the water overflow to reach the surface of the fish/bridge, made of steel grating painted blue, momentarily covering it, while slowly receding. Lit from below, this piece will glow at night. There are spaces for 455 cars.

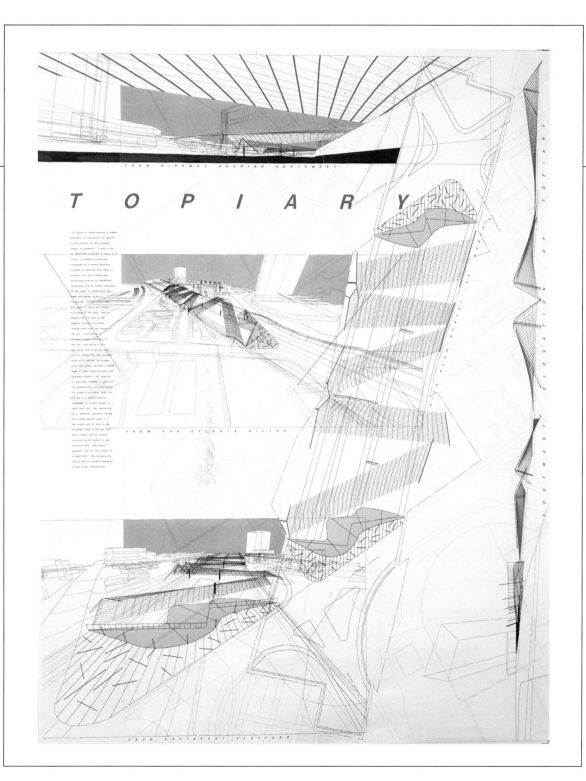

Competition Board. The Topiary is a figurative allusion to landscaping practices. In this case, mounds are created with red chain-link, partially covering the great void in the city created by the highway below.

Fierstein Residence

BROOKSVILLE, MAINE

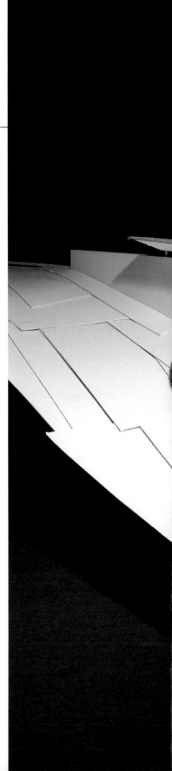

Here we must think of everything at once:

Lisa Fierstein and her body, her shadow, a big eye opening,

A ritual similar to a strip-tease,

To seek for a moment of silence. (The site did not offer it), it was too noisy, in spite of the view,

and retaining walls, somewhere between landscape and architecture: these thoughts became a dance, a pentagram,

a way to inscribe another topographical accident among those found. An endorsement.

More than a project of architecture, this is a landscaping exercise: the initial task was to arrange a sequence of retaining walls to establish the desired relationship between view and rooms, subsequently determining the changes in levels most akin to use and circulation. The rooms are conceived as various frames overlooking the scene and culminating in the living-dining area where the most favorable vistas are exposed through a long, elongated, and oversized arch as a single opening. Since the site is heavily wooded the rooms are generously dimensioned to allow for spaces not available in the natural realm, mostly occupied by trees and shadows. The roof is thin, understood as a soft mantle laid over the walls, which are solid, made of stone, and firmly attached to the topography.

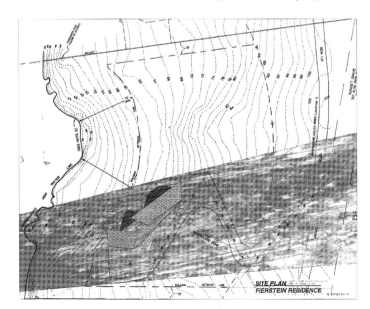

SITE PLAN
FIERSTEIN RESIDENCE

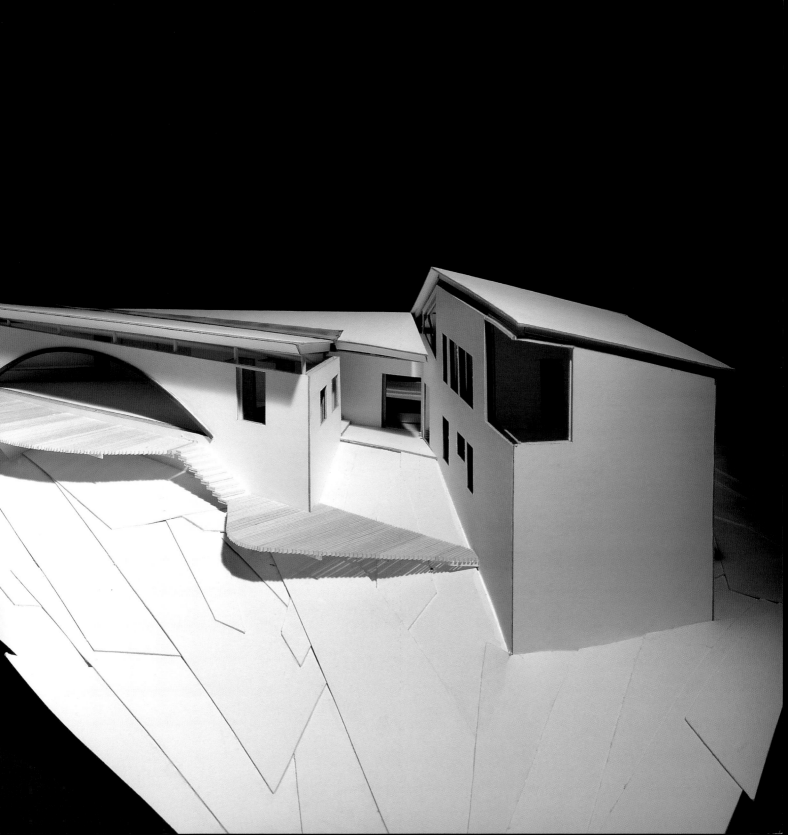

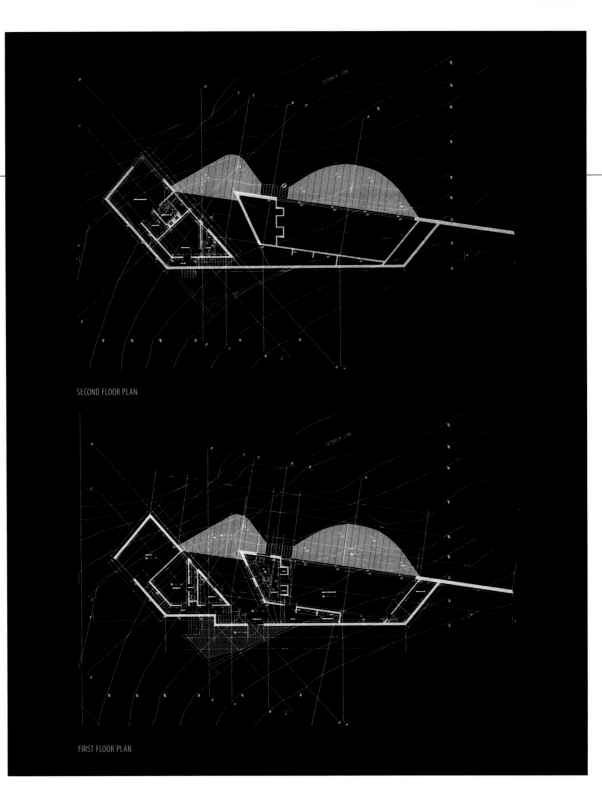

SECOND FLOOR PLAN

In the study sketches, interior spaces understood as "clearings" of the site, and the main framing of the views through the big eye in the living room. Rather than completely opening to the view, it was intended to articulate the openings "in crescendo" toward the living room and the master bedroom (opposite page).

FIRST FLOOR PLAN

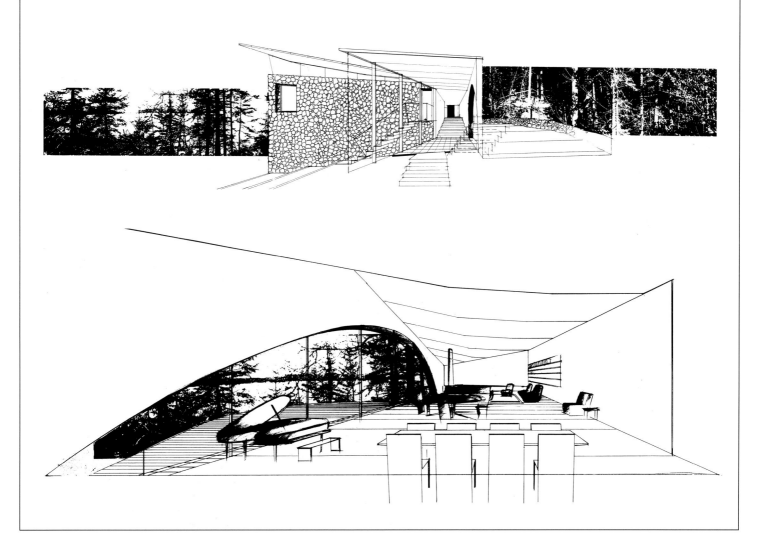

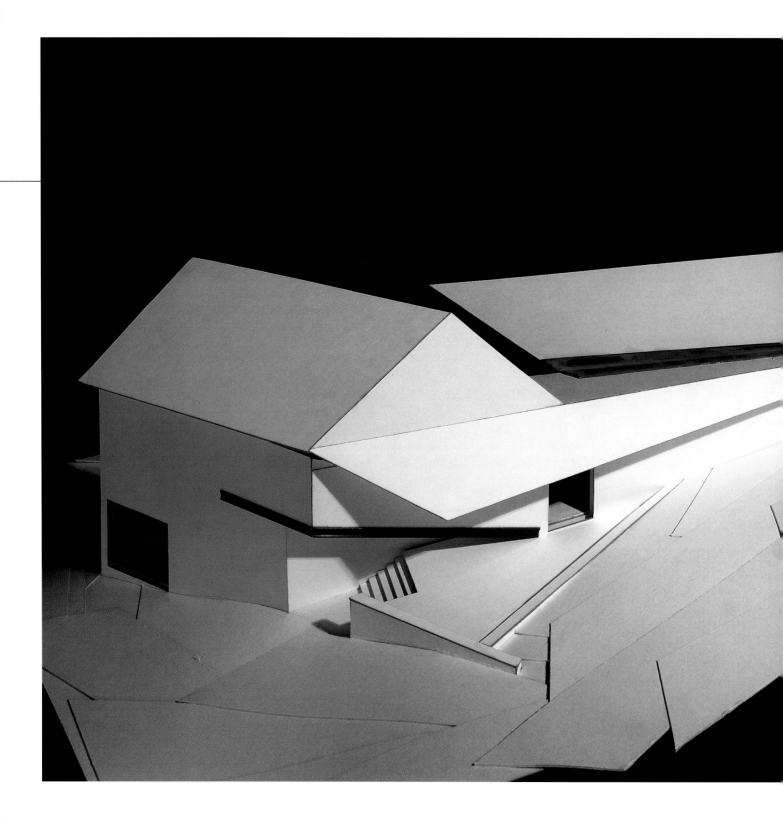

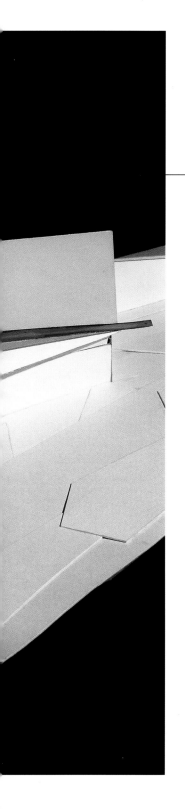

SOUTHWEST ELEVATION

NORTH ELEVATION

BEDROOM ELEVATION

SOUTHEAST ELEVATION

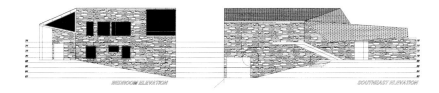

EAST ELEVATION

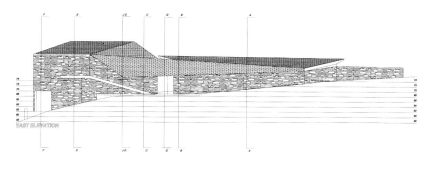

Elevations/model showing the
relationship of the heavy (stone)
walls, conceived as retaining walls
in the landscape, and the light
(asphalt shingles) folded roof,
understood as a soft mantel
covering the retaining walls.

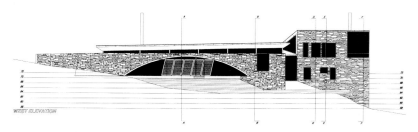

WEST ELEVATION

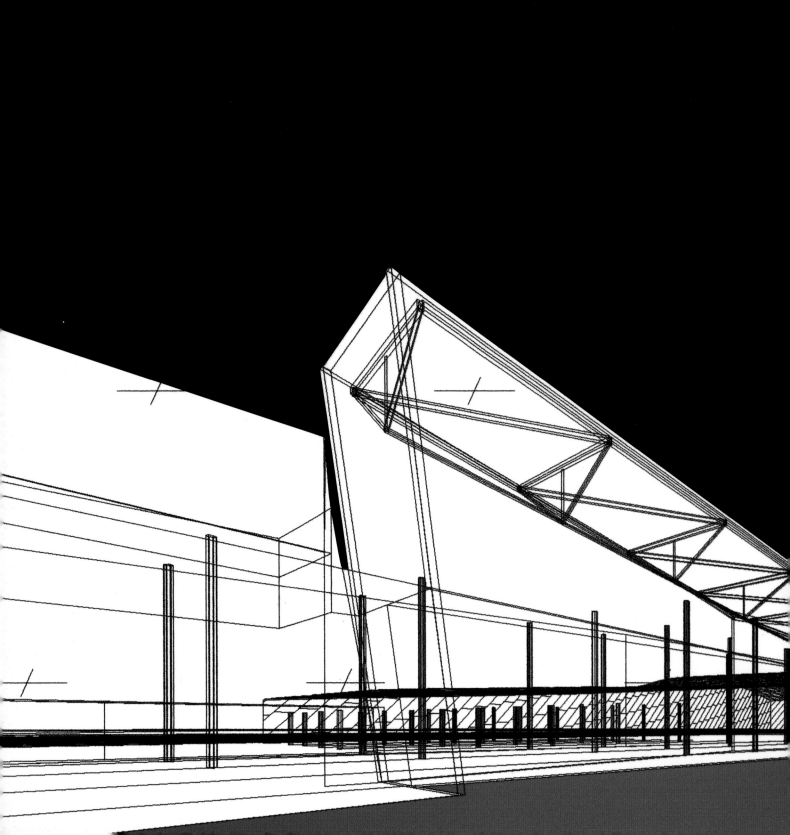

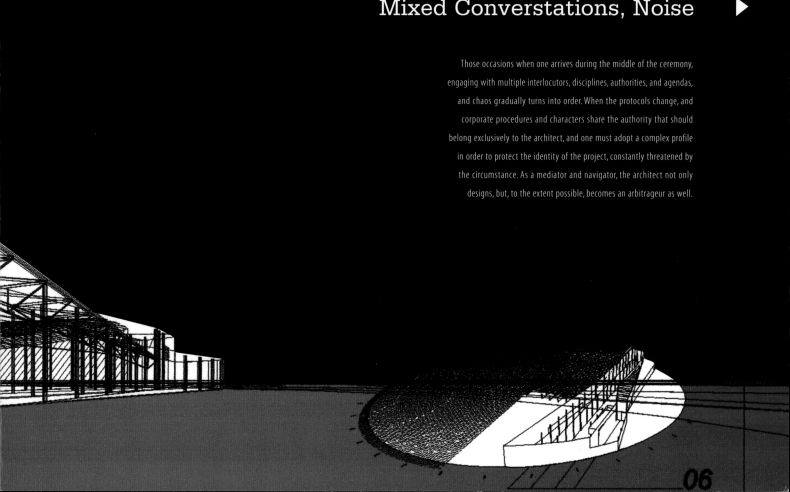

Those occasions when one arrives during the middle of the ceremony,
engaging with multiple interlocutors, disciplines, authorities, and agendas,
and chaos gradually turns into order. When the protocols change, and
corporate procedures and characters share the authority that should
belong exclusively to the architect, and one must adopt a complex profile
in order to protect the identity of the project, constantly threatened by
the circumstance. As a mediator and navigator, the architect not only
designs, but, to the extent possible, becomes an arbitrageur as well.

06

found in "Butler" buildings, the custom-made structural steel ribs show the profile of a large piece of furniture, or an object, in this case in the middle of the field.

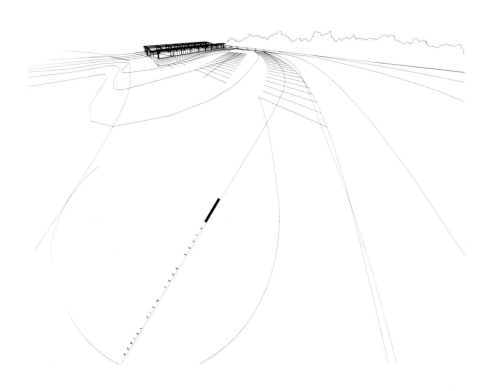

AERIAL VIEW FROM SOUTH

The project borrows from pre-engi-
neered building systems, establishing
a repetitive structural pattern, in this
case made of custom fabricated "I"
beams and columns with rigid-moment
connections. This proved to be less
expensive, actually, than off the shelf
systems. The roof is standing seam metal.

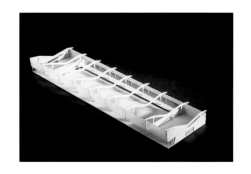

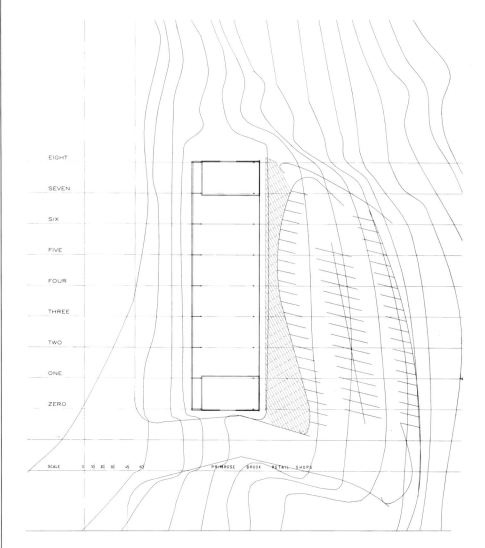

EIGHT

SEVEN

SIX

FIVE

FOUR

THREE

TWO

ONE

ZERO

SCALE   0   10   20   30   45   60   PRIMROSE BROOK RETAIL SHOPS

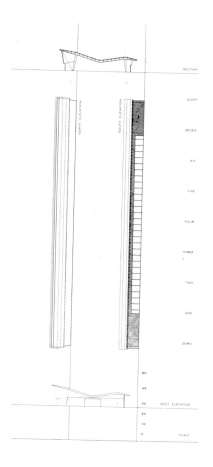

SECTION

EIGHT

SEVEN

SIX

FIVE

FOUR

THREE

TWO

ONE

ZERO

80

45

30   WEST ELEVATION

20

10

0   SCALE

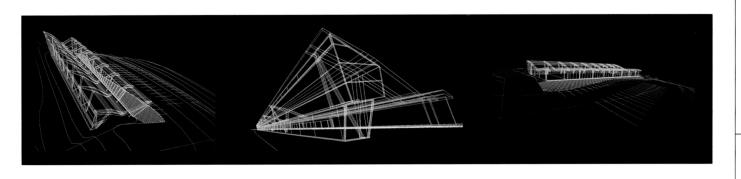

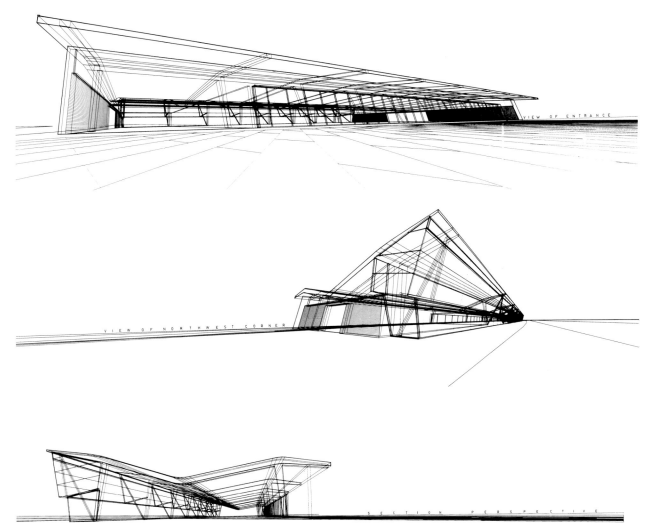

VIEW OF ENTRANCE

VIEW OF NORTHWEST CORNER

SECTION PERSPECTIVE

BCRA/Operations Center

Located as a single object in a park, strict setbacks, accessibility, and height restrictions forced the occupation of the buildable area almost in its totality. Special consideration was given to the presence of an elevated highway from which the roof of the building would be visible.

The history of a project is often paradoxical. In this case, it certainly doesn't start at the beginning, instead it is associated to decisions that precede its origin, as in a case of simulation or disguise. Here it happened when an unforgiving program generated by strict adjacencies was paired by a two-sided site pretending to be a circle. Sky and horizon must, for once, be apart in Argentina. High security requirements demand so. To understand that was very helpful. After that, it seemed only logical to divide the building into two main pieces, one for the working areas, the other for the storage of gold and currency. Here the roof is clad in stainless steel, a big shield visible from the highway. There, the sky becomes a huge window. Little more can be said of the project as a whole. We must wait for the acute observer to gather—through perception more than language—that which the profession is never able to delineate and that architecture, through mysterious paths, often congregates.

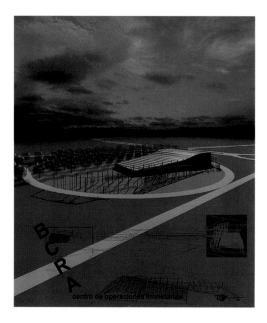

BCRA

centro de operaciones monetarias

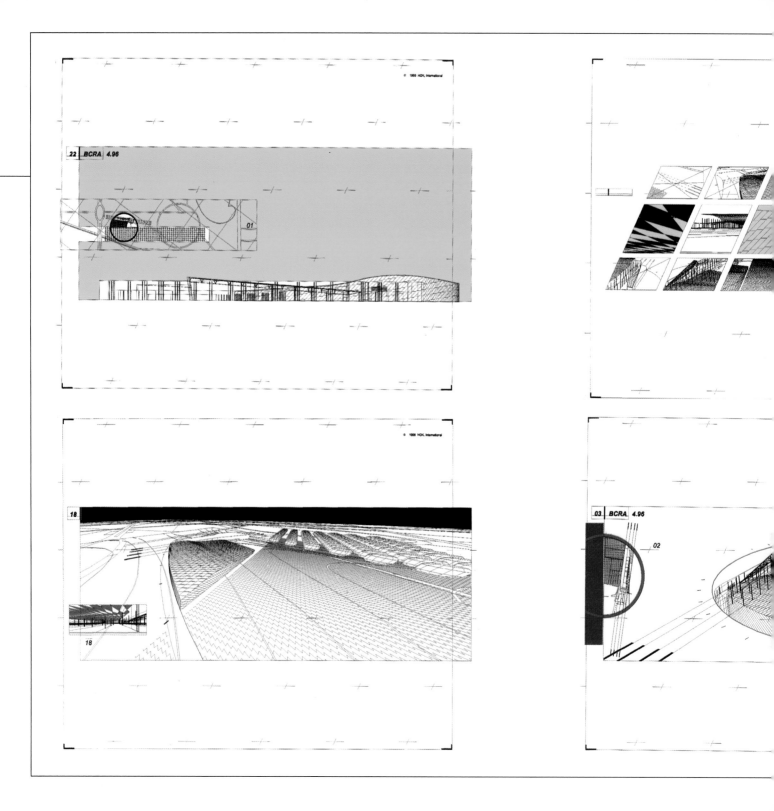

22 BCRA 4.96

01

18

18

.03 BCRA 4.96

02

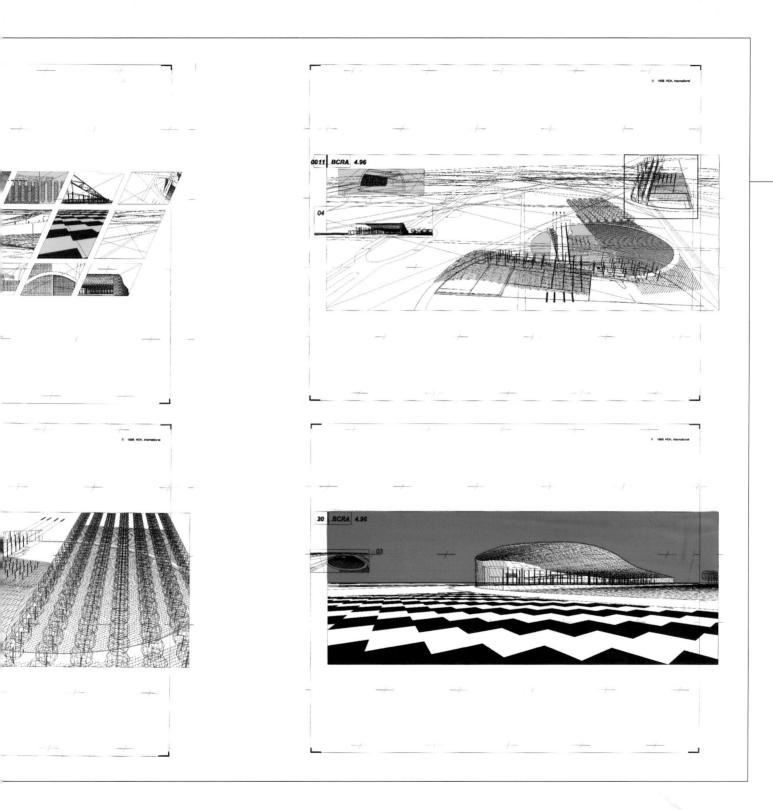

0011 BCRA 4.96

04

20 BCRA 4.96

03

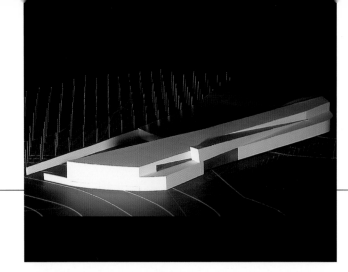

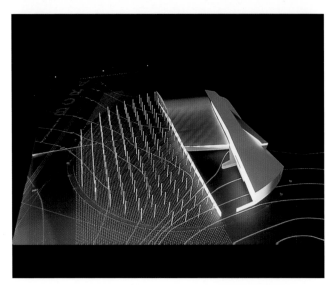

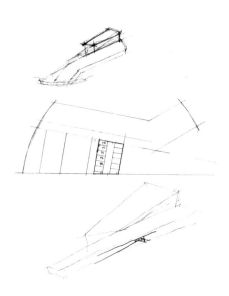

Views of the model showing the two main volumes of the project, the vaults area and the offices area (this page). The roof of the vaults (opposite page) is clad in stainless steel panels of different finish. Due to its position, it would be visible from a nearby highway.

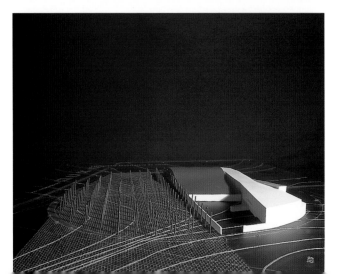

World Omni Building

Located on a four-acre (two-hectare) parcel of an office development, the position of the building on the site divides the land in its two main uses: required parking (380 cars) and work area. Since this was a suburban structure whose main approach would be from the parking lot, we opted to place the building sideways with respect to the entry road.

Off the shelves: Because it was a speculative office building, a general economy (conceptual, technical, formal, functional, budgetary) informed the project. Consequently, it was important to find a dimension applicable to all fundamental demands of space allocation: cars and people. The same bay is used to organize parking slots, workstations, and structure. Conceived as a strip of utilitarian space too long to fit in the site, the "L" shape of the plan achieves two goals: It creates a partially enclosed garden-court on the north side, and it maintains a bay depth sensitive to the employees.

The only portion two stories high is the entrance lobby, behind which the mechanical spaces hide above the roof. This also allowed for the extension of the roof, creating a large canopy that marks the entrance on the south side.

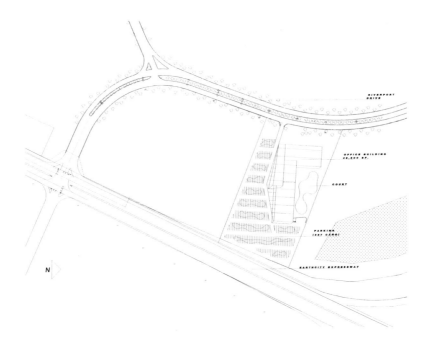

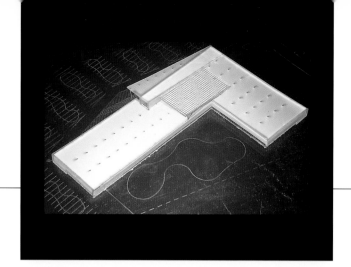

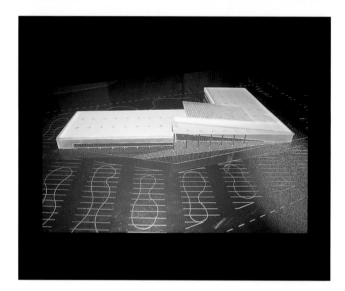

Plan showing the strategy to understand the arrangement of space as a continuum, where an equal system organizes the structural bays of the building and the parking slots in the parking lot. This borrows from agricultural practices, where markings in the land allow for its appropriation for different uses. This is also a commentary on suburban sprawls, where the markings in the land change from agricultural to architectural (opposite page).

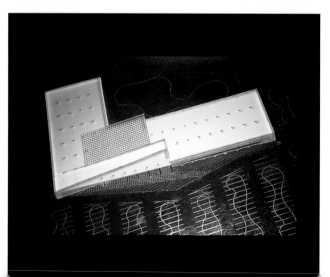

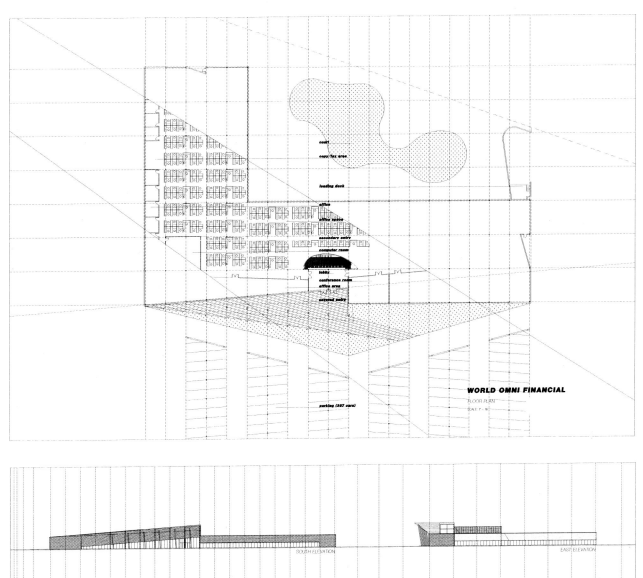

court
copy/fax area

loading dock

office
office space
secondary entry
computer room
lobby
conference room
office area
covered entry

parking (287 cars)

WORLD OMNI FINANCIAL

FLOOR PLAN
SCALE 1" = 16'

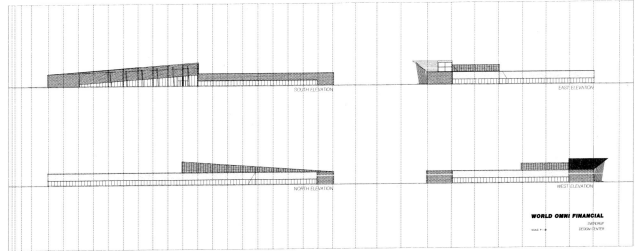

SOUTH ELEVATION

EAST ELEVATION

NORTH ELEVATION

WEST ELEVATION

WORLD OMNI FINANCIAL

SCALE 1" = 16'

SVERDRUP
DESIGN CENTER

Costantini Museum

The fundamental concept informing the project is the desire to value the horizontal over the vertical, associated with the South American, pre-Hispanic devotion to the land as an ulterior principle (Pachamama), also understood as the concept of "basesse" (Bataille), privileging the monumental as the non-erect. The site is divided by a single line along its longitudinal axis that organizes the spaces and accommodates the program through a number of minimally sloped ramps useful to circulate, to exhibit art, to be an auditorium floor, and to park cars. This economy of articulation also permits an equal distribution of spaces, based on dimensions adept to various modes of arrangement for specific exhibits, be they painting or sculpture. Additionally, by merely covering the existing roof of the third level, the future expansion (required) can be accommodated. Counter to this motion a fast ramp—similar to a tango step, a "firulete," permits for a quick exit-descent without having to return through the path of ascent.

The exterior walls of the building will be made of a light panel system ("Kalwall"), translucent and able to distribute natural diffused light in equal amounts to the exhibition spaces. In this regard, the same quality of light is achieved, eliminating complex skylights and special detailing. Randomly placed columns support the ramps, and the space can be subdivided by translucent canvas stretched among the columns, creating virtual rooms while maintaining the overall continuity of the space. The solid (ramps) remains in the horizontal planes, the vertical (walls) is conceived as ethereal. This also allows the museum to glow at night, further revealing the presence of the ground ascending.

To conclude, this museum is an occasion to create a topography more than a monument, a "combinatoire" of gestures informed by the rotation of the vertical axis (which typically organizes the construction of a monument) onto a horizontal landscape-dimension that congregates and embraces specific modes of perception, spaces, architecture, art.

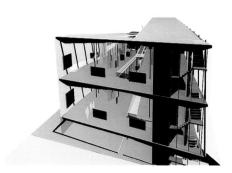

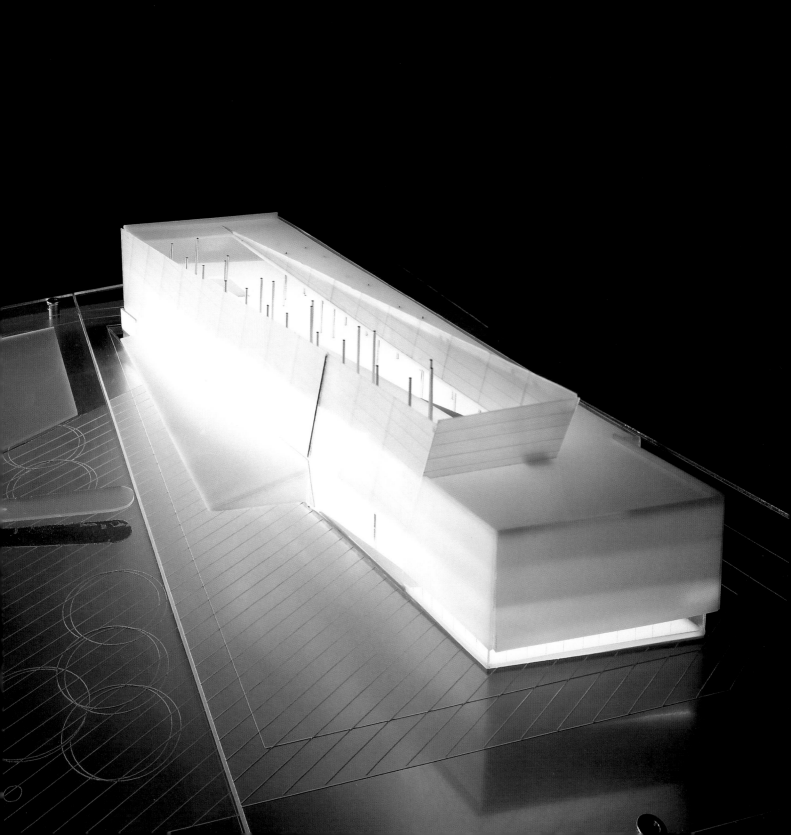

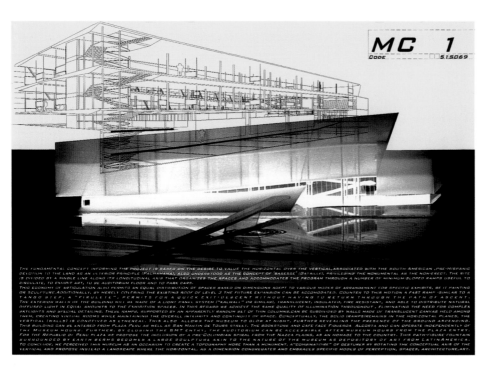

MC 1
CODE 515069

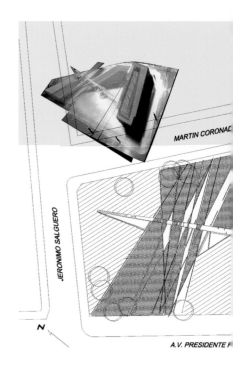

MARTIN CORONAD

JERONIMO SALGUERO

N

A.V. PRESIDENTE F

THE FUNDAMENTAL CONCEPT INFORMING THE PROJECT IS BASED ON THE DESIRE TO VALUE THE HORIZONTAL OVER THE VERTICAL, ASSOCIATED WITH THE SOUTH AMERICAN, PRE-HISPANIC DEVOTION TO THE LAND AS AN ULTERIOR PRINCIPLE (PACHAMAMA), ALSO UNDERSTOOD AS THE CONCEPT OF "BASENESS" (BATAILLE), PRIVILEGING THE MONUMENTAL AS THE NON-ERECT. THE SITE IS DIVIDED BY A SINGLE LINE ALONG ITS LONGITUDINAL AXIS THAT ORGANIZES THE SPACES AND ACCOMMODATES THE PROGRAM THROUGH A NUMBER OF MINIMUM-SLOPED RAMPS USEFUL TO CIRCULATE, TO EXHIBIT ART, TO BE AUDITORIUM FLOOR AND TO PARK CARS.
THIS ECONOMY OF ARTICULATION ALSO PERMITS AN EQUAL DISTRIBUTION OF SPACES BASED ON DIMENSIONS ADEPT TO VARIOUS MODES OF ARRANGEMENT FOR SPECIFIC EXHIBITS, BE IT PAINTING OR SCULPTURE. ADDITIONALLY, BY MERELY COVERING THE EXISTING ROOF OF LEVEL 3 THE FUTURE EXPANSION CAN BE ACCOMMODATED. COUNTER TO THIS MOTION A FAST RAMP -SIMILAR TO A TANGO STEP, A "FIRULETE", PERMITS FOR A QUICK EXIT -DESCENT WITHOUT HAVING TO RETURN THROUGH THE PATH OF ASCENT.
THE EXTERIOR WALLS OF THE BUILDING WILL BE MADE OF A LIGHT PANEL SYSTEM ("KALWALL" OR SIMILAR), TRANSLUCENT, INSULATED, FIRE RESISTANT, AND ABLE TO DISTRIBUTE NATURAL DIFFUSED LIGHT IN EQUAL AMOUNTS TO THE EXHIBITION SPACES. IN THIS REGARD WE ACHIEVE THE SAME QUALITY OF ILLUMINATION THROUGHOUT, ELIMINATING THE NEED FOR COMPLEX SKYLIGHTS AND SPECIAL DETAILING. THESE RAMPS, SUPPORTED BY AN APPARENTLY RANDOM SET OF THIN COLUMNS, CAN BE SUBDIVIDED BY WALLS MADE OF TRANSLUCENT CANVAS HELD AMONG THEM, CREATING VIRTUAL ROOMS WHILE MAINTAINING THE OVERALL INTENSITY AND CONTINUITY OF SPACE. CONCEPTUALLY, THE SOLID (RAMPS)REMAINS IN THE HORIZONTAL PLANES, THE VERTICAL (WALLS) IS CONCEIVED AS ETHEREAL. THIS ALSO ALLOWS THE MUSEUM TO GLOW AT NIGHT, FURTHER REVEALING THE PRESENCE OF THE GROUND ASCENDING.
THIS BUILDING CAN BE ENTERED FROM PLAZA PERU AS WELL AS SAN MARTIN DE TOURS STREET. THE BOOKSTORE AND CAFE FACE FIGUEROA ALCORTA AND CAN OPERATE INDEPENDENTLY OF THE MUSEUM PROPER. FURTHER, BY CLOSING THE SMT ENTRY, THE AUDITORIUM CAN BE ACCESSIBLE AFTER MUSEUM HOURS FROM THE PLAZA ENTRY.
FOR THE REPUBLIC OF PERU PLAZA WE PROPOSE THE INCLUSION OF A PRE-COLUMBIAN SPIRAL FROM THE NAZCA PLAINS, AS AN HOMAGE TO THE COUNTRY. THIS PATH-FIGURE FOUNTAIN SURROUNDED BY EARTH BERMS BECOMES A LARGE SCULPTURE AKIN TO THE NATURE OF THE MUSEUM AS DEPOSITORY OF ART FROM LATIN AMERICA.
TO CONCLUDE, WE PERCEIVED THIS MUSEUM AS AN OCCASION TO CREATE A TOPOGRAPHY MORE THAN A MONUMENT, A "COMBINATURE" OF GESTURES BY ROTATING THE CONCEPTUAL AXIS OF THE VERTICAL AND PROPOSE INSTEAD A LANDSCAPE WHERE THE HORIZONTAL, AS A DIMENSION CONGREGATES AND EMBRACES SPECIFIC MODES OF PERCEPTION, SPACES, ARCHITECTURE, ART.

MC 4
CODE 515069

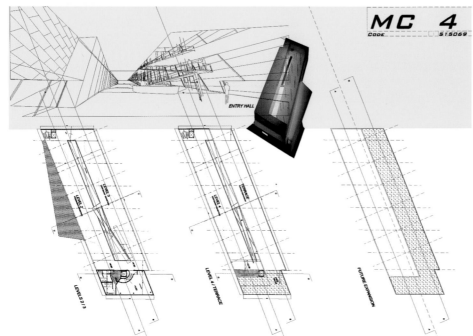

ENTRY HALL

LEVELS 2/3

LEVEL 4/ TERRACE

FUTURE EXPANSION

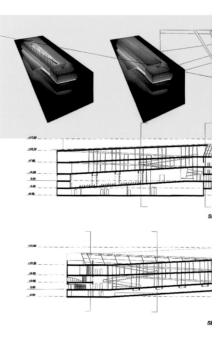

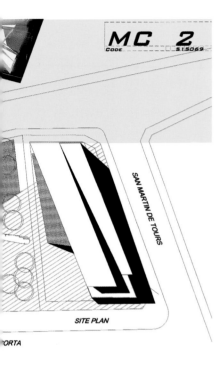

MC 2
CODE 5.1.5069

SAN MARTIN DE TOURS

SITE PLAN

PORTA

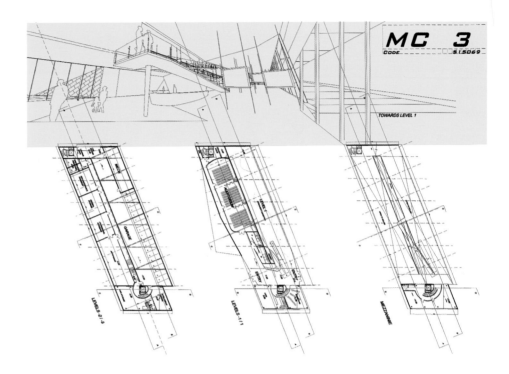

MC 3
CODE 5.1.5069

TOWARDS LEVEL 1

LEVELS 2/3

LEVELS -1/1

MEZZANINE

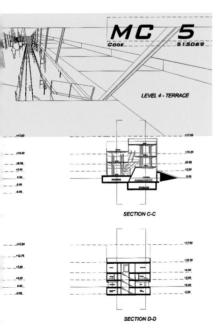

MC 5
CODE 5.1.5069

LEVEL 4 - TERRACE

SECTION C-C

SECTION D-D

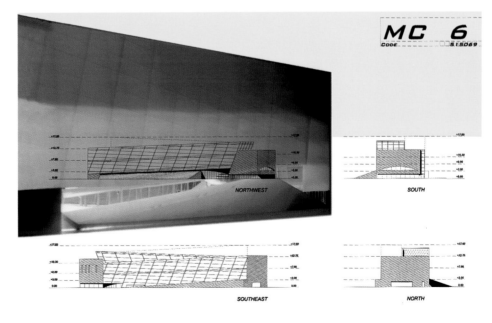

MC 6
CODE 5.1.5069

NORTHWEST

SOUTH

SOUTHEAST

NORTH

Costantini Museum

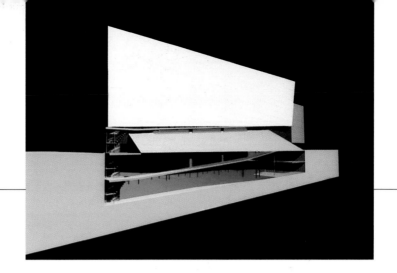

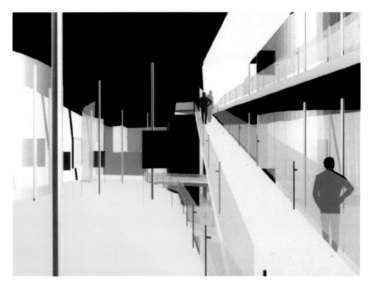

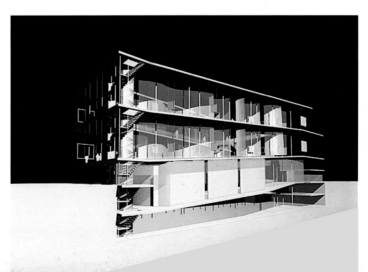

Studies showing the slow ramps, designated for exhibition and viewing and the fast ramp, for quick exiting, within the plan layout. This counterplay of slow and fast movement is inspired in the "firulete," a tango step.

Multimodal

Situated at the northern edge of the site, this Concourse building faces exceptional views of downtown St. Louis. Additionally, it can be seen from the Interstate 40 elevated highway. Within these parameters, the building is exposed significantly to either the car or pedestrian, thus becoming a significant piece within the built context. Its footprint is informed by the motion of the traffic flow, and its two fundamental components, the eastern façade and the roof, endorse the complex urban conditions previously mentioned. The east façade, perceived from the Metrolink ramps, the Kiel Auditorium, and the westbound pedestrian, will have the role of a "gate" into this complex. By appearing as a vertical single plane made of glass and extruded polycarbon panels, it will glow at night, becoming a true marker for the site.

The roof, made of standing seam panels curving on the west side, suggests motion and enhances the formal attributes of the building, its proportions on this side of the site suggesting the image of a train. At the north edge, a terrace overlooking downtown follows the pedestrian ramp toward 15th Street. To the south the building becomes a concourse linkage with the Amtrak/Greyhound Terminal. This linkage continues the formal principles of the Concourse building, with a glass façade on its eastern side and a curved metal roof to ensure continuity.

By sitting along the Metrolink railroad line, these buildings define the edge of a large open area and instill it with a strong architectural character, bringing to the site a concrete sense of place. And as connectors between Metrolink, bus, railroad and car, they are simultaneously a gate, a hall, a balcony, and a window into St. Louis.

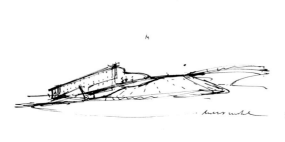

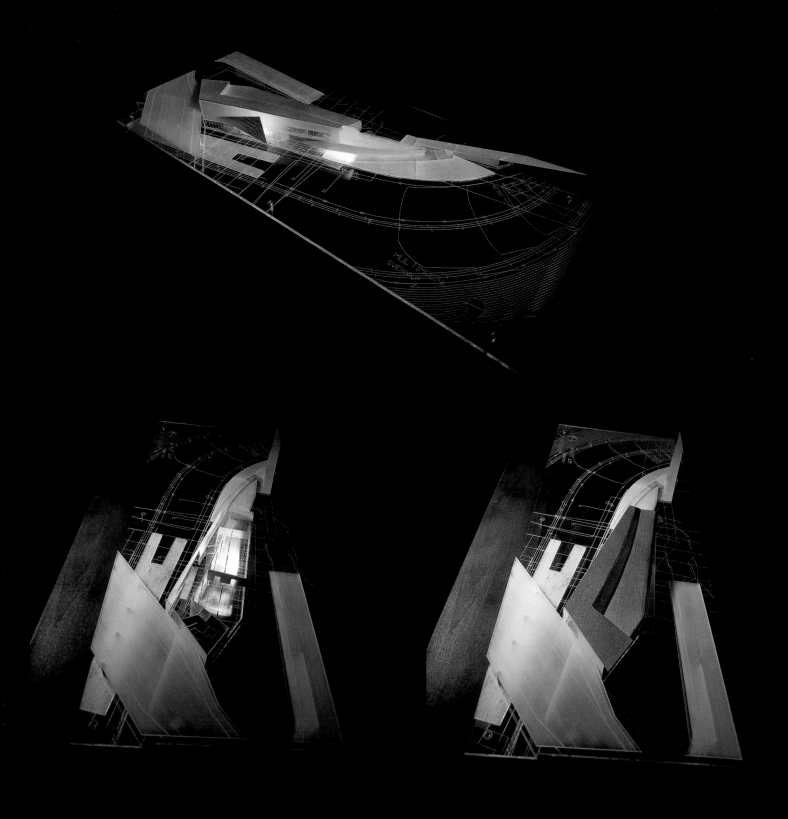

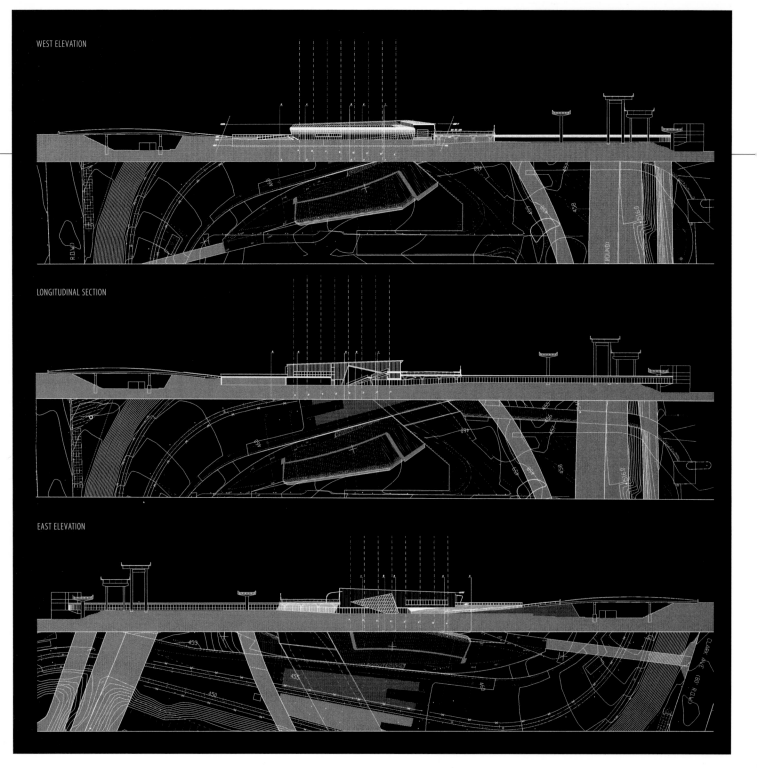

WEST ELEVATION

LONGITUDINAL SECTION

EAST ELEVATION

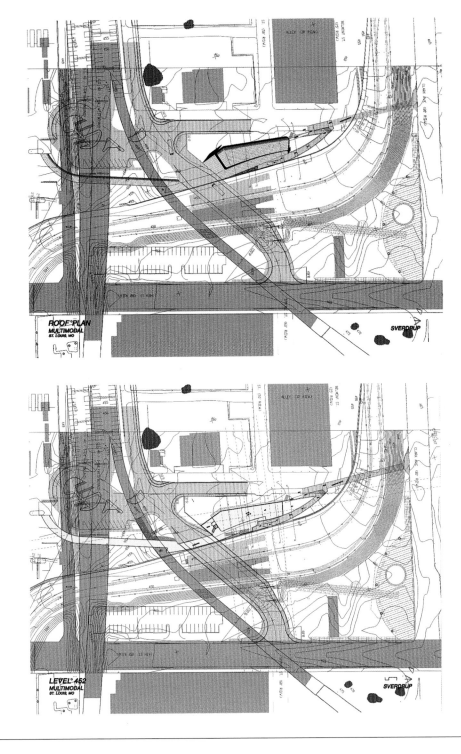

Roof plan and plan showing all formal
"layers" of information, trajectories, and
pathways within the site: highway, street
extension, Metrolink, streets, on- and
off-ramps. The sections (opposite)
show the various levels of connection
through the building.

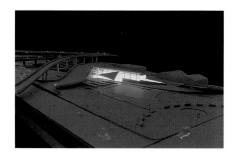
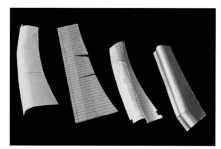
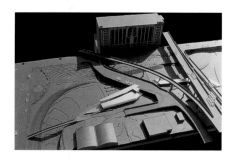

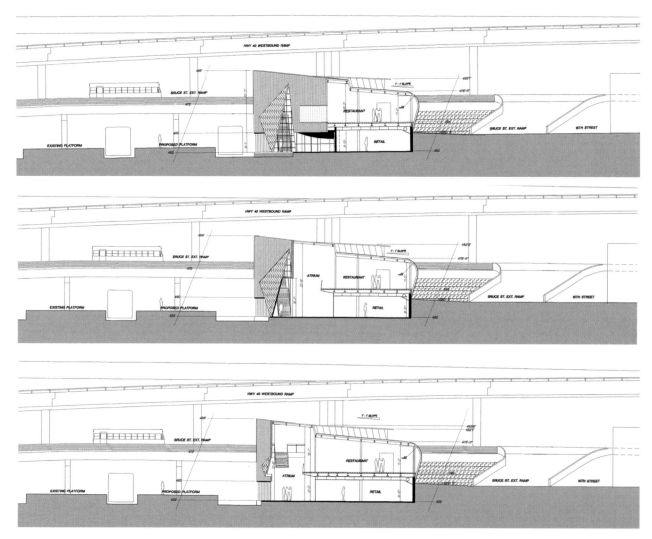

DRAWINGS: EAST—WEST SECTIONS; STUDY MODELS: NIGHT VIEW(LEFT), ROOF(CENTER), AERIAL VIEW(RIGHT); PHOTOMONTAGE: DAY—NIGHT

Appendix ▶

List of Works and Credits

COOPER BAUER APARTMENT
Boston, Massachusetts 1988–89
Client: Michael Cooper, Nancy Bauer
Architects: Denison Luchini Architects
Assistants: Hunter Fleming, Mark Koeninger, Michael Moran
Model: Adrian Luchini
Contractor: Balance One Inc., Boston, Mass.
Photographs: Jon Jensen, originally published in *Metropolitan Home* Magazine,
a publication of Hachette Filipacchi Magazines, Inc.; Adrian Luchini, Dirk Denison

HEILIG RESIDENCE
St. Louis, Missouri 1989–90
Client: Dr. & Mrs. Robert Heilig
Architects: Schwetye Luchini Architects, Inc.
Assistants: Matthew Forman, Lisa Kincaid
Model: Adrian Luchini
Photographs: Adrian Luchini

PIKU RESIDENCE
Detroit, Michigan 1990
AIA Design Excellence Award, 1994
Client: Mr. & Mrs. Frank Piku
Architects: Denison Luchini Architects
Assistants: Michael Pierry, Cecilia Perez, Matthew Read
Model: Matthew Read
Contractor: Frank Piku
Photographs: Balthazar Korab, Wayne Fujii (Archimage), Adrian Luchini

MARITZ-STAREK RESIDENCE
St. Louis, Missouri 1990–1991
Client: Alice Maritz & Karel Starek
Architects: Schwetye Luchini Architects, Inc.
Assistants: Matthew Forman, Lisa Kincaid, Matthew Read
Model: Matthew Forman, Adrian Luchini
Contractor: G & L Contractors, P. J. Prifti Co., Vulcan Metals Co.
Photographs: Sam Fentress, Adrian Luchini

HEMATIAN RESIDENCE
Long Island, New York 1993
Client: Effi Hematian
Architects: Schwetye Luchini Architects., Inc., Adam Kalkin, Associated Architect
Assistants: Matthew Forman, Gisella Vidalle
Model: Gisella Vidalle
Photographs: Bob Pettus

CAMP BEERSHEBA CHAPEL
Beersheba Springs, Tennessee 1996–1999
AIA Design Excellence Award, 1998
Client: Board of Directors, United Methodist Church
Architects: Sverdrup Facilities, Inc. Adrian Luchini, Director of Design,
Curt Lambdin, Project Manager, William Hummel, Structural Engineer
Assistants: Don Fedorko, Terry Oden, Mike Bell
Model: Taro Narahara
Photographs: Peter Wilson

THE ARMS OF MANHATTAN
New York City, New York 1987
2nd Prize, Manhattan Waterfront International Competition
Architect: Adrian Luchini
Assistant: Bobby Loh
Model: Peter Wolf
Photographs: Adrian Luchini

KDNL-TV/THE FOX
St. Louis, Missouri 1991
Client: River City Television Partners
Architects: Schwetye Luchini Architects, Inc.
Assistants: Matthew Forman, Elizabeth Kincaid
Contractor: Spiegelgass Construction Co.
Photographs: Renee Gregg

SIXTH CHURCH OF CHRIST, SCIENTIST
St. Louis, Missouri 1992
AIA Design Excellence Award, 1993
Client: Board of Directors, Sixth Church of Christ, Scientist
Architects: Schwetye Luchini Architects, Inc.
Assistants: Matthew Forman, Ben Fuqua
Contractor: Metropolitan Design and Building
Model: Adrian Luchini, Matthew Forman
Photographs: Sam Fentress, Adrian Luchini, Bob Pettus

KOPLAR RESIDENCE
St. Louis, Missouri 1992
Client: Mr. & Mrs. Ted Koplar
Architects: Schwetye Luchini Architects, Inc.
Assistants: Matthew Forman, Ben Fuqua, Gisella Vidalle, Sajja Mayalarp
Model: Sajja Mayalarp
Photographs: Bob Pettus

ATLANTA COMPETITION
Atlanta, Georgia 1994
Architect: Schwetye Luchini Architects, Inc.
Assistant: Sean Ahlquist

FIERSTEIN RESIDENCE
Brooksville, Maine 1997–2000
Client: Dr. and Mrs. Jeffrey Fierstein
Architect: Adrian Luchini
Assistant: Steve Brabson
Model: Sajja Mayalarp
Photographs: Bob Pettus, Adrian Luchini

NEW JERSEY RETAIL
New Jersey 1994
Client: Eugene Kalkin
Architects: Schwetye Luchini Architects, Inc., Adam Kalkin, Associated Architect
Assistant: Sean Ahlquist
Model: Gisella Vidalle ·
Photographs: Bob Pettus

BCRA/OPERATIONS CENTER
Buenos Aires, Argentina 1995
Clients: Banco Central de la Republica Argentina
Architects: HOK Architects, St. Louis, Adrian Luchini, Senior Designer,
Michael Haggans, Project Manager, David Chassin, Programming
Assistants: Don Fedorko, John Major, Jeremy Roach, Randolph Miles, Charlie Neer
Model: Randolph Miles
Photographs: Randolph Miles

WORLD OMNI BUILDING
St. Louis, Missouri 1996
Client: World Omni International
Architects: Sverdrup Facilities, Inc., Adrian Luchini, Director of Design,
Joel Wexelman, Project Manager
Assistants: Terry Oden, Mike Bell, Don Fedorko
Model: Terry Oden, Mike Bell
Photographs: Tony Carosella

COSTANTINI MUSEUM
Buenos Aires, Argentina 1997
Architects: Sverdrup Facilities, Inc., St. Louis, Adrian Luchini, Director of Design
Rozenwasser, Silverfaden Associated Architects, Buenos Aires, Argentina
Assistants: Don Fedorko, Terry Oden, Taro Narahara, Mike Bell
Model: Taro Narahara
Photographs: Don Fedorko

MULTIMODAL
St. Louis, Missouri 1997–1998
Clients: City of St.Louis
Architects: Sverdrup Facilities, Inc., Adrian Luchini, Director of Design,
John McCarthy, Project Manager
Assistants: Don Fedorko, Terry Oden
Model: Takesshi Namba
Photographs: Peter Wilson

From left to right: Terry Oden, Adrian
Luchini, and Don Fedorko

ACKNOWLEDGMENTS

I owe much to Oscar Riera Ojeda for his untiring, patient support and interest in my work.

To Enric Miralles and Lauren Kogod for their invaluable insight.

To Dirk Denison, the ideal partner.

To Thomas Schwetye, from whom I learned the fundamental tips to survive in the Midwest.

To Washington University and Dean Weese, for their enthusiasm for the Professor-Practitioner formula that allowed me to pursue my vocation in full.

To my parents, who educated me.

DEDICATION:
To my children,
and especially to Magda, que es todas las mujeres.